P. POLICY

VOLUME I

A story & self help book on setting boundaries and maintaining Self Respect

Thank you, Cal
Sovereign Jane Jenkins

Sovereign Jane Jenkins

Pussy Policy Volume I

A story & self help book on setting boundaries and maintaining self-respect

If you don't know who you are,

people will treat you according to who THEY think you are.

Sovereign Jane Jenkins

Copyright

Copyright © 2023 by Sovereign Jane Jenkins

All rights reserved.

No portion of this book may be reproduced, stored in a retrieval system, or transmitted in any form or by any means, electric, mechanical, photocopying, recording, scanning, or otherwise, without written permission from the author and as permitted under sections 107 or 108 of the 1976 United States Copyright Act, without either the prior written permission of the publisher or authorization through payment of the per-copy fee to the Copyright Clearance Center:

Requests to the Publisher or Author for permission should be addressed to Sovereign Jane Jenkins at jjenkins@inursecoach.com.

Limit of Liability/ Disclaimer of Warranty: While the publisher and author have used their best efforts in preparing this book, they make no representations or warranties with respect to the accuracy or completeness of the contents of this book and specifically disclaim any implied warranties of merchantability or fitness for a particular purpose. No warranty may be created or extended by sales representatives or written sales materials. The advice and strategies contained herein may not be suitable for your situation. You should consult with a professional where appropriate and indicated. Neither the publisher nor the author shall be liable for damages arising therefrom this work.

For privacy reasons, some names, locations, and dates may have been changed.

Cover Photography by Albee

Book Cover design by Awan Designer

1st edition 2023

Title: P. Policy: A story & self-help book on setting boundaries and maintaining self-respect

Sovereign Thinkers LLC

Identifiers: 979-8-9891748-0-5

Subjects: LCSH: Self Help. | Personal Memoirs.

Dedication

I would like to dedicate this book to every woman in the world who has made mistakes and grown from them. However, we need to normalize learning from other people's experiences so that we don't fall victim to the trials, traumas, and tribulations that life brings by going through the same things. This book is for every woman to learn from someone else's mistakes, including myself.

I'm human.
I'm faulty.
I'm honest.
Now,
I'm free.

Take what you can from these lessons…

Thank you ,Mama, for giving me everything that you could most of my life, for you bubble-wrapped and protected me from the rest of the world. You always kept me next to you and protected me from everything that you could until you couldn't….. I'll always love you for that.

Thank you ,Dad, for the hard life lessons in life. They were necessary for my growth and made me who I am today. Not so shabby for your DNA.

As you can tell, writing this book was like opening an old scar with a butter knife, but it's necessary for my healing process to eclipse and reach completion .This is my story, and I'm shedding all of my filters.

The good…
The bad…
The ugly…

This is also dedicated to every woman questioning her intuition and life decisions.

Table of Contents

Chapter 1: Introduction	1
Chapter 2: Privacy Invasion	4
Chapter 3: Church	11
Chapter 4: The Cookout	19
Chapter 5: Lessons from the Rearing	26
Chapter 6: Taking Chances	31
Chapter 7: Dangling the Fruit	37
Chapter 8: Falling in Love	48
Chapter 9: True Colors	60
Chapter 10: The Thanks We Give	65
Chapter 11: Pussy is a Privilege	73
Chapter 12: The Gift of Giving	83
Chapter 13: Relationship-Phobic	88
Chapter 14: Valentine's Day	100
Chapter 15: Game Night	110
Chapter 16: The Aftermath	129
Chapter 17: 'Cuffin' the Soul	144
Chapter 18: A Walk of Completion	153
Chapter 19: She Loves Me, She Loves Me Not	167
Chapter 20: A Love Lost	175
Chapter 21: The Accident	182
Chapter 22: The Settlement	186
Chapter 23: Poker Face	194
Chapter 24: The Messages	207
Chapter 25: The Curse of Death	218
Chapter 26: Gia's Warning	224
Pussy Policy	235
About the Author	236

Chapter 1

INTRODUCTION

As I sat across from my pseudo-sugar daddy, Carter, quietly as he read the news on his phone, one question kept cycling through my mind. I studied him intently while sitting in bed. Carter was exactly twice my age at fifty. I knew he was sitting on a wealth of knowledge and wisdom; I wanted to know the big secret that only men knew.

"What did you mean by that question you asked me yesterday?" I asked intently.

"What question?" He said, looking up at me, pausing to read the article on his phone.

"The question about my 'pussy policy'?" I asked, digging into his psyche.

He seemed to laugh out loud at my naivete. I wasn't joking, and the question was far from funny.

"Baby, listen…," he said as if I were his child.

"Most women don't have any standards or boundaries, and they let men run through them like a marathon.., " he paused momentarily, " You see, a hospital has a policy in place for their staff to protect the hospital in case the staff strays from the policy and coincidentally cause a near miss or a sentinel event to a patient, whether it was done through sheer ignorance or purposefully, the hospital is still not at fault. So the staff will face the consequences regardless, right?" He said as his eyebrow quirked my way.

I nodded, not knowing exactly where he was going with this train of thought.

"If a hospital has by-laws to protect themselves, why don't most women? Women have more to lose as an individual than a corporation. They can catch every STD in the book. They can get pregnant. They can be used and abused. Yet, they still let the average Joe with half a brain emotionally destroy them and piss on their self-esteem," He continued.

I continued to gawk at him, feeling uneasy. 'Those women' whom he was referring to were once me, so I kept my mouth slammed shut.

"Why? Because they have no boundaries or system of self-government to protect themselves. Many women are lost and rely on a monthly child-support check from a dude who wants nothing to do with them, but they are still chasing that same man while he's dragging them through the dirt." Carter said.

"But what does that have to do with me?" I asked.

"I was checking to see if you would tell me how to get you going. I wanted you to tell me how to crack your code without doing the work to learn it the hard way. I wanted to see how stupid you were," He said unflinchingly.

I blinked at his brutal honesty while he continued to tell the plays from the Players' Handbook.

"Men are lazy by nature, after all. We aren't looking for love. We never really have because we rarely love. We're looking for what purpose you could serve," he said, turning back to his phone after shattering my perceptions about both men and love.

"So it was a lie. You never loved me," I said knowingly.

He looked up at me once more. "You already knew that. That's why you still haven't given me your 'pussy policy.' I tell you, 'I love you,' and you just stare at me silently, knowing I'm full of shit. You're a hard one to crack. At least you're a challenge," he said thoughtfully. I laughed disingenuously. We had both been burned so much that we could read each other quite well. He was right; I didn't love him at all. We were simply using each other. I glanced at the brand-new watch he'd bought me and saw it was nearly one o'clock in the morning. 'Time to rest,' I thought as my head hit the pillow. No more questions were needed. The revelation in my mind was clear. I understood everything I would ever need to know about the game.

Chapter 2

PRIVACY INVASION

An eye for an eye makes the whole world blind.
*~ **Mahatma Gandhi***

Dallas, Texas
August 31, 2019

Twenty-two years a virgin... Twenty-two years gone down the drain for this... I loved Gandhi's quote, and it had been my favorite since the seventh grade. However, I couldn't help but dream about snatching the man's eyeballs from their sockets and stomping on them until the white substance oozed out. The *grown man* in the next room of course, not Gandhi. I sat on the closet floor, hyperventilating, hands shaking, heart pounding in my ears, and eyes straining to see the rest of the text messages in the darkness.

Pussy Policy #1: Never invest more than you're willing to lose in a relationship.

I wanted blood. I wanted the air permeated with the iron-fragranced liquid. My heart was slowly breaking, and there was nothing that I could do to stop it. I could not turn back. I could not unread the messages, the messages that confirmed that what I believed for two years was actually the truth, the messages that confirmed my worst fears, the messages that proved to me what kind of a person I was truly with: selfish, inconsiderate, flawed, and a liar......

Messages sent the previous weekend:

Her: I really cannot stand you. We literally just discussed this.
Me: Would an apology help?
Her: Don't apologize, but your energy keeps changing...For example, after you hugged me your energy turned cold...but I'll understand whether you chose her or me. Regardless, make sure you find happiness in the end and stop trying to force me to be ok. That's not how grieving works. I still would like to remain friends.
Me: I'm very tired.
Her: I don't see how. You fell asleep quickly after.
Me: I could have gone for round 2...
Her: My bad...
Me: What's that for?
Her: If I wasn't there, you could've gotten proper rest...
Me: That's not a fact.
Her: Maybe... Regardless, my apologies!
Me: My balls are sore.
Her: Why?
Me: Doggy style...
Her: The final thrust hurt?
Me: Yes...
Her: Ok. Not on purpose. Not trying to harm you, I promise.
Me: Hopefully the swelling goes down.
Her: It definitely should by the end of today.
Me: I hope so... For my sake at least.
Her: Word.

Me: Did you finish?
Her: The question is: Did you finish???
Me: Again, another round would have been nice.
Her: Yet, you fell asleep. Lol. I finished, but another round could have happened.
Me: Fair enough.
Her: You know I get buck wild when tipsy…

The more I read, the more I began to shake.

In a world full of Malcolm Xs, I always chose to be Martin, but Martin's movement evaded me on this day.

How DARE this man? He had all the audacity but no tenacity. The rage that I tried to tame was sharply building in my core and was coming to the point of spilling over. I was too hurt even to cry. All I felt was that out-of-body experience of fury while he slept peacefully on the couch in the next room after our late-night sex session; of course, he fell asleep afterward. I felt sick to my stomach. I bet my bottom dollar he didn't use a condom. He complained every time I wanted to go back to using condoms. He would always say that he couldn't feel it. I didn't feel a ring on my finger, so I didn't care what he could or couldn't feel. This particular time, we didn't use a condom, and I was mortified. I was a healthcare professional. I knew the risks. I knew better, BUT I didn't do better.

Pussy Policy #2: If he's not your husband, make him use a condom because loyalty isn't always a valued attribute in relationships.

The very thought of him made me ill as I listened to him snore while I finished reading the text messages.

Messages from two days ago:

Her: I'm coming this weekend, Can I crash? Or do I need to stay elsewhere?

Me: Yes. You do. Why this weekend? Neka's coming through this weekend and isn't leaving until Monday.
Her: Oh. Ok, then. It was good that I did come this past weekend in the end then...
Me: Yes, her schedule isn't set, so it's hard to plan it out around her coming and going. That's very true.
Her: Things happen for a reason... Any who, shoot me a list of things to do while I'm there, so I won't text you while she's near you. I want to have a blast not thinking about you and her.

Now, I wasn't one to believe in calling people "bitches"; it was a degrading, cynical term that I despised. But... she was the epitome of the term! Both she and he fit the label perfectly! They were both entirely reprehensible, and they would feel my wrath. That was both a promise and a curse. For me, it was the sheer principle of the matter. I felt like someone had doused me with a bucket of ice water. The shock was palpable as I sat on the closet carpet, as vulnerable as a bird, expecting this man to propose to me soon. After all, I had not only given him my most prized possession—my virginity—but I had also supported him when a freak car accident had left his foot broken in half. I could have abandoned him when he was at his lowest—broke, injured, without a car, house, or job. That would have been my moment to leave him without looking back. Yet, my empathetic side couldn't bear to leave him at his lowest, even though he had called his ex-girlfriend, Rene, to the accident scene after I missed his call. I was at work, navigating my first week of orientation.

Pussy Policy #3: Don't let empathy turn you into someone's victim.

My blood was boiling so avidly that my face felt like an inferno as I read on...It was like Satan himself was blowing his pungent breath into my face while whispering in my ear to harm him in his slumber, to end his life for what he did to me. I smiled at the sheer stupidity while thinking of how sweet it would be to see the blood pour out of his neck like a spout. I read on further…

Her: THANK YOU! I really appreciated the money.
Me: No problem! However, we need a code word from now on.
Her: Ok, what's the word
Me: Ask me,' what's up', and if I don't say "the sky, no lie!" It's not me. We had an argument and she mentioned texting you. I can't really explain.
Her: Fair enough. Sounds good!
Him: Awesome! Thanks for understanding and being a friend.
Her: No, thank you for sending the money. The girls need some new school uniforms. I appreciate it.
Him: No problem. I got you.

Pussy Policy #4: Do not give up ALL your benefits to a boyfriend; love is a gamble, but don't risk it all.

I would have fallen right out of it if I had been sitting in a chair at that moment. This man had tried every excuse to avoid giving me a penny from his hundred-thousand-dollar accident settlement, yet he freely gave her money. No way! I had to threaten to leave him just to get him to pay for my car radio, trips, and hotel room expenses after I shouldered those costs alone for so long during his handicap from shattered metatarsals I actually laughed out loud at that. I wasn't sure if it was genuine amusement or sheer disbelief, perhaps a mix of both. But one thing was clear: I was so incensed that I couldn't see straight. He was truly trying to lead a double life with his ex on the side. I thanked God I had heeded my mother's advice. She had told me never to cook for him, clean for him, wash his clothes, or, most importantly, give him money. I washed his clothes once, and after his complaints, I never did it again. I never gave him money, never cooked for him, and certainly never cleaned for him. One should never let someone exploit them. Always ensure you're the one who comes out ahead. **Before anyone receives such**

benefits, they must prove they're worthy of being a husband—both in actions and title—before you become their wife in any sense.

I was in a state of disbelief…

Oh, No..No..No. That simply won't do.

I heard my phone beep in the next room, indicating the reception of someone's message. I stood up on wobbly legs and walked out of the closet. I strolled around the apartment looking for something that would cause pain without killing: the glass cup could kill him, the frying pan would make too much noise and possibly kill him, and the iron would most likely cause a traumatic brain injury. I don't even think I could have pleaded insanity at this point because my mind was overanalyzing everything as a weapon. I stopped in front of him and stood over him. For how long, I don't recall. I looked at him with pure disgust and disdain, thinking of doing the worst of sins. Two years of my life…my virginity…my money…all gone to waste. A man that my family disapproved of, a man that my father would have disapproved of, and a man that I wholeheartedly disapproved of at that very moment. I could hear all the 'I told you so from my two older brothers, mother, and stepfather.

No, there was no turning back. The pressing question was: What should I do next? Do I confront him and risk entering the Texas jail system, jeopardizing my nursing degree, and tarnishing my career over this mess I was unexpectedly 'thrust' into? (No pun intended.) Alternatively, do I simply turn away, count it as a loss, and consider it a lesson learned? I didn't want to just walk away. All that training, coaching, discussions, and planning for the future would amount to nothing—just a colossal waste of time with only a broken heart to show for it.

He slept peacefully, unaware, as a wild look took over my face. I glimpsed my reflection in the mirror above the couch. It felt as if another side of me was urging me on, pushing me to end the pain, to make him pay for what he believed he could get away with. My life flashed before my eyes: every part of who I was, all the trauma I'd experienced, the highs and lows, converged like trains on multiple tracks. Every moment thudded in my mind, its rhythm matching the pulsing beat in my ears, synchronized with my racing heart. I remembered my graduation day from just eighteen months ago. Standing on stage, I was adorned with the title "magna cum laude," with numerous sashes and medals draped around my neck. The weight of those honors now mirrored the heaviness of the moment. The burden of betrayal was almost tangible. Though I was bare, I felt an overwhelming heat engulfing me. Shifting my gaze from the mirror, I saw him lying on the couch, his carotid artery pulsing rhythmically as he slept. I held his phone tightly. I knew that the trajectory of my life hinged on this moment. With a heavy sigh, I placed his phone on the coffee table, grabbed mine from the kitchen counter, and dialed my mother. She was the voice of reason I could always rely on, my trusted advisor. At 2:00 a.m., as expected, she was awake.

"He cheated on the bed that I picked out with his ex-girlfriend," I rambled once I heard her voice on the other end of the phone.

She paused, "Janeka, listen to me. Pack all your things and go to your aunt's house right NOW!" I could hear the edge and urgency in her tone. My heart was racing, and I felt sick to my stomach. I wanted vengeance. I wanted blood. I could feel my blood boiling in the pit of my stomach. The food that I had eaten earlier threatened to make an appearance. I got angrier as his snoring grew audibly louder. I was hurting while he was sleeping. That was the joke of the century, but that joke was totally on me while he was oblivious at the moment. So, the number one golden rule flashed through my psyche like a wheel of fortune and stopped at the golden rule:

Pussy Policy #5: Never tolerate cheating without serving a real consequence.

Chapter 3

CHURCH

"Church…The place where we come to heal our hurts…
But also the place that hides the most dirt…
Church..The place that boasts of healing our souls…
But also the place that houses the most foes..."
~Sovereign Jane Jenkins

Jackson, Mississippi
April 23, 2000

It was Easter Sunday, so it was a huge deal. Church on a Sunday was customary for black people in Mississippi. We prayed our way through so many battles. That's how we got through slavery, Jim Crow laws, and the Civil Rights movements. Not belonging to someone's church was almost criminal if you lived here. That's where we sought healing. When my mama was hurting and in pain, she took us to church. But only when she was hurting. We weren't the *church every single Sunday* type of family. Sometimes, the church would last the whole day. After twelve hours of worship, you'd think we all knew every scripture in the Bible by then. That was the Mississippi way for us 'black folk.' People's blood sugar would drop from the lack of food, children would fall asleep for the lack of understanding, and old women would fan themselves while screaming, "Yes, Pastor!" even though their hands were numb from the constant clapping.

Sometimes, it felt like a spectacle. I'd usually never get the message.

What was the point of it all?

We donned our finest suits, fragrances, loafers, gators, hats, tambourines, and fans for church services. At times, it resembled a fashion show more than a religious gathering. The older ladies always carried large purses stocked with tissues and peppermints, although these bags often smelled of mothballs. They typically wore long dresses paired with low-heeled shoes. Pants for women were strictly forbidden. This was life in the Church of God in Christ or COGIC for short. The praise and worship dancers performed their pantomime routines with grace and precision, moving in harmony with the song's rhythm. Their movements radiated passion, fervor, and a palpable sense of the divine.

The routines often portrayed life's challenges weighing us down, yet we persisted, always finding a way through. We've always endured. I once performed a routine where I hammered the floor with my hands and knees, depicting a world filled with pain, sorrow, and suffering. The essence of the performance was overcoming that darkness, confronting challenges head-on, and persevering against adversity. We never backed down when faced with obstacles; we doubled our efforts and pushed on.

Being young, I hadn't experienced all the world's sorrows. I was mostly trying to understand why my father was absent. Communication with him ceased, and our weekend visits became a thing of the past. It felt as though he'd vanished, and no one could provide an explanation. I knew he wasn't dead. I prayed to God, pleading for my father's return to our lives. That was my deepest wish. My prayers always culminated with a heartfelt "Amen!"

I looked around at all the other kids in church to see if they were also praying. They weren't. I guess they had their daddies around.

I looked at the pastor of the church, Pastor Allen. He would sweat profusely while shouting scriptures and explaining the points of them. I still didn't understand his gusto.

"Lord, help me provide healing over your people tonight. We need you, Lord! We need YOU!" Pastor shouted!

"Yes, Lord!" I'd hear his wife say as she sat to the right of the stage. She was lighter skinned with a pink hat and a shiny broach. She had long, thick black hair; she was a beautiful woman. Mama thought she was on the stuck-up side, so I never spoke to her. I looked over to her children. There were three of them. They appeared bored like every other child in the room. Maybe they weren't praying like I was because they had their daddy around.

" When the lord walks in….." Deep nasal breath…Cue the organ.

"The devil gets scared…" Deep nasal breath…Cue the organ.

"Cause the devil knows!!" Deep nasal breath…Cue the organ.

"That he's no match for the God I serve!" Deep nasal breath…Cue the organ.

"Cause the Lord is my savior!" Deep nasal breath…Cue the organ.

"And you will not win, devil!" Deep nasal breath…Cue the organ.

"I said you will not win, Devil!" Deep nasal breath…Cue the organ.

"Can I get an 'amen!'"Deep nasal breath…Cue the organ.

"Cause I don't think y'all hearing me!" Deep nasal breath…Cue the organ.

"I said, ' Can I get an Amen!'" Deep nasal breath…Cue the organ.

"Cause y'all too quiet for me!" Deep nasal breath…Cue the organ.

"Cause Lord!!!!!!!!!—" Deep nasal breath…Cue the organ and the drummer, and we head into a praise and worship song headed by the sweating pastor.

>"Ooh, Lordt'!
>
>You are the King and ALMIGHTY!
>
>And to you, I will SING!
>
>I had to get up out of my SEAT!
>
>To let you know that you are KING!
>
>Praise you!
>
>Cause we are FREE!
>
>And we're going to continue to praise you!
>
>Until the wind is gone from our WINGS!"

I sat there wide-eyed like a doe in front of humans.
What in the church is going on in here? I thought silently to myself.

I don't know if I felt more empowered or more scared, but Mama said, "Amen!"
So, I clapped my hands as if I knew what he was talking about.

Pussy Policy #6: Choose a partner with similar foundational beliefs and values as you: religion, politics, practices, and wellness regimens.

I looked to my right to find my cousin, Sisi, trying not to fall asleep. How could she sleep at a time like this? This man could wake up the Devil in hell by the way he's screaming. She was used to it, I realized. Sisi was two years older than me. Her mother was my Auntie Royce. Auntie Royce and my mother looked like twins, but they were five years apart, with my mother being the older of the two; they never seemed to get along that well, either. Auntie Royce and Mama were sitting at the front of the church while we were two rows back because the kids tended to fall asleep, and they didn't want the preacher to see us sleeping. It was dishonorable.

I glanced at Pastor Allen's children and noticed his son was nodding off. Sisi seemed to feel the same way. Their drowsiness amused me, but I nearly leaped from my seat when the Pastor, in all his enthusiasm, jumped onto the front pew and then leaped off as if he were an acrobat, all while passionately delivering his sermon. I figured they'd be passing the tithing plates soon, given that everyone was thoroughly entertained and alert by that point. Even Sisi, previously dozing off, was now staring at the preacher, her eyes wide with astonishment. Sisi had an older sister named Sunday, whom we affectionately called Sunny. Sunny was at the front of the church with our mothers.

I looked back over at Pastor Allen's children; the oldest daughter rolled her eyes, looking like she would rather be anywhere but there; she was darker skinned like her father. Her younger sister was bigger than her but fairer-skinned than her. She had a bigger head, too, but that wasn't a nice thing to think. I turned my gaze back to their mother as she fanned herself in the front of the church, appearing lady-like like a first lady should. She held an air of honor yet arrogance about her. I guess it came with the territory. Being a first lady in Mississippi was like being a local celebrity. Everyone knew you, and everyone knew your business. That wasn't a place that I cared to hold. Give me a commoner who loves the lord and is graciously humble at the same time, but not a preacher.

I sighed, thinking about my father. I hadn't talked to him in a few months. He and Mama were fighting again, especially after she nearly threw a brick through the front windshield of his car after she found out he had another woman in the house where we all used to live. I didn't understand why there was so much hostility between them. If it meant they wouldn't kill each other, I was all for the divorce and separation. A chill went over my spine as I recalled Mama coming home from the hospital with black and blue bruises decorating her body and a broken nose in three places. She looked like she had gotten in a car accident. As it turned out, Mama and Daddy had gotten into their final fight, which forced their divorce and official break-up. I remembered that day like it was yesterday…

Three years prior

"Daddy, where are you taking us?" I asked while playing with my doll Rapunzel. He looked spaced out as he rambled about, grabbing my brother's and my night clothes. I guess we were headed over to Grandma's for the weekend. We spent a lot of time at her house. She practically helped raise us.

"Come here, Janeka," he said, picking me up by my underarms. I held on to his neck as my older brother came running down the hallway with his Power Rangers action figure and his pjs that matched. Daddy seemed very angry, but he placed me patiently into my car seat when we reached the car. Chayne jumped into the back seat on the opposite side of me. I held onto Rapunzel, and he held on to his Power Ranger. A storm was brewing outside the car as we drove to Grandma's in complete silence. The day had turned cloudy and gloomy, but the rain hadn't started just yet. Daddy was usually fair-tempered and cool. He had a playful and peaceful aura when he wasn't drunk or angry. I loved my Daddy very much despite his imperfections. Once we arrived at Grandma's, he picked me up from the car seat.

"Janeka. Chayne. I love y'all very much," he said, placing me on my feet and kissing both of us on the forehead. He dipped into the car once more and grabbed my diaper bag.

"Chayne, help your grandma with Janeka, and don't forget to bathe tonight," he said, walking us to the door.

Grandma was waiting with the door wide open. I ran to her and hugged her leg. I turned back around and realized that Daddy was already in the car, pulling away from Grandma's house.

Chayne walked into the house first, and then I followed. I guess we'll be watching her stories all weekend. Once we were safely inside, the rain started pouring, the thunder cracking against the house like a whip. Grandma turned off the TV.

"We don't watch TV while the lord's working," she said in fear, looking towards the roof of the house.

I looked up, too. "Lord! Let my daddy make it home safely," I prayed silently. I hoped that I was doing it right. Mommy said to pray to the lord for your wishes to come true, so that's what I did. I didn't know where Mommy was, but I hoped she was someplace safe, too. I looked back at Grandma. She was a round, thick, almond-colored woman with long white hair. She had gout in her lower legs and walked with a cane around the house. She also didn't have any teeth, but she made the best biscuits in the world. I couldn't wait to get started on helping her with dinner. She had a worried look on her face as she stared out of the window into the storm brewing outside. I was short and couldn't quite reach the window sill, but I walked towards it anyway and stood on my tippy toes, trying to see out of it. I watched as the drops of rain pounded the pavement. I felt strangely unsettled as I held onto Rapunzel tighter.
"Janeka, get away from that window," Grandma said in her first warning to me that weekend.

Pussy Policy #7: Never allow physical abuse in your relationship. Leave after the first instance.

I blinked, the memory fading as quickly as it had surfaced. I surveyed the church once more, recognizing many members who had been attending for years. It often seemed as if they came to church seeking a savior, as if their salvation hinged entirely on their faithful attendance to every service. What troubled me about the Church in the south was how deeply people embedded their faith in religion, often leaving little faith in themselves. There seemed to be no genuine sense of 'KNOWING' or 'DIRECTION'. The primary focus appeared to be regular church attendance and tithing, yet there was often a lack of guidance on tangible steps to personal salvation. It felt as though prayer was the solution to everything. Yet, many of our ancestors prayed tirelessly, and still, many of them faced hardships until their unfortunate demise inevitably came. I'm not arguing against prayer; rather, I believe in the power of pairing prayer with actionable steps. I wouldn't advise someone to pray for a million dollars and then simply continue their same daily routine, hoping for a financial windfall. Life doesn't operate on mere wishes. **Effort is always necessary!**

Pussy Policy #8: Whether you have a man or not, have your own sense of direction and put in work towards it.

Chapter 4

THE COOKOUT

"As long as my body has breath, the truth shall ring free from my womb to the devil's dismay."
~Sovereign Jane Jenkins

Collins, Mississippi
April 10, 2005

The cookouts in Mississippi were a staple for us on a Sunday afternoon. Destressing after a long week was always on the agenda. There was loud music, barbeque, long tables of food, and people everywhere with matching t-shirts and little babies. There was also dancing. Lots of twerking…It was a cultural dance, a way to celebrate where we came from to where we are today.

"Shake It Like A Dog" by Kane & Abel came on, and everyone rushed to the dance floor to cut a rug. The energy was infectious, especially when the female cousins began rolling their hips in their short shorts, prompting the males to try their best to look away. It was comical, but the fact was, the females really could dance, regardless of their attire. Everyone was laughing and thoroughly enjoying themselves. This particular cookout held special significance as it celebrated Granddaddy's birthday. There was an added layer of enthusiasm, given the circumstances. Though Granddaddy was gravely ill with cancer, no one let the mood dip that day. It was a full-blown party, and even Grandma made an appearance, despite her and Granddaddy having been divorced for decades.

"Man, cousin! If you weren't my cousin," I heard one of my male cousins say.

I laughed because everyone was just that transparent and straightforward.

"Man, take your nasty-behind somewhere and cool off. This ain't Alabama," one of my other female cousins said with sass and neck-rolling.

"Man, 'she' the one wearing them shorts," my cousin Leon said, defending himself.

I began to tune out my cousins as I observed the entire scene. I was silent like a monk but observed everything around me like a sponge.

The older great uncles were at the table playing dominoes and spades while arguing and talking about the 'good ole days.' *Whatever that meant..*

All of my aunts and uncles were there. My grandmother had eight children: Auntie Floyd, Auntie Denise, Auntie Ruby Mae, Auntie Sarah Lee, Mama, Auntie Royce, Uncle Tim, and Uncle Jay. Those were the children my grandparents had together. My Auntie Denise was the second eldest, but she died before I was born. My grandfather had additional kids with other women during the course of their marriage: He had Auntie Linda, Uncle Lenny, Uncle Brandon, and a few others that I've never met or heard of. It was common for men back then to have outside kids. It was almost a rite of passage, but certain women weren't putting up with that shit. Unfortunately, my grandma had dealt with it for years before washing her hands of the situation. Granddaddy's outside women would even go so far as to drop their kids off randomly with her for the weekend, and she'd take care of them for the weekend while Granddaddy was off in a completely different woman's drawers. It was a hard life for Grandmother. I looked at all my aunts and uncles with grateful hearts, but I couldn't help but wonder about the kind of hell that my grandmother went through during their marriage. It pained me to even think about it. Yet, she stood there, still jolly and strong like a stone pillar.

Pussy Policy #9: Never tolerate a man having a child with another woman during your relationship with him.

Grandma was a meek woman who had suffered immensely over the years. Granddaddy once left her for another woman, despite her desperate pleas for him to stay, all in front of their young, impressionable children. He even dragged her along the driveway of their home as she tried to stop him, but it was in vain. Papa was a rolling stone, always on the move. Despite all the pain she endured, Grandma never appeared bitter; she seemed at peace. A God-fearing woman, she leaned on her faith, especially growing up in 1900s Mississippi, where that faith was a lifeline. Grandma worked as a maid for the affluent in Jackson. Over the years, she witnessed much, heard countless stories, and was given many labels. Yet, she never lost her joy. Her patience was extraordinary, but even she reached her limit, eventually divorcing Granddaddy after enduring his years of infidelity. As I passed by, I heard her infectious laughter and could spot her gleaming gold tooth even from across the sunlit yard. It signified her delight in something. Grandma had tales to tell, and I hoped to hear them someday. My lingering question was, "Why did she stay for so long?"

I shrugged as I walked by, watching everyone's exchanges. I was nine years old then, and I could see through everything. I walked by Granddaddy, and he looked like a shell of his former self. He was a smoker and smoked for years, so he had emphysema and lung cancer. I grew sad; I didn't want to remember him like this; I loved my granddaddy. I wasn't ready to say goodbye. I sighed as I spotted Sisi further up the driveway. She was playing basketball with my other cousins. I walked up the pathway to her. She was standing with my other cousin, Sky.

As I came into view, Sisi dropped the ball to hug me. She was my closest cousin. We were basically raised together.

After I hugged her, I pulled back to hug Sky.

Sky acted like I didn't even exist.

"Sky, hug your cousin," said Sisi.

"I don't want to hug that fat ass girl!" Sky exclaimed.

My stomach sank through my spine at that moment. Her words deeply hurt me, and I wasn't sure where the animosity came from.

"Sky! What's wrong with you? That's your family!" Sisi said sharply.

Sky halfway hugged me against her true wishes.

My self-esteem had plummeted to an all-time low. I had a belly, but I wasn't fat-fat. I was nine and still growing into my body.

"Ignore her, cuz!" Sisi said, lifting my chin back up. I was sad, but Sisi wouldn't let my chin fall for a minute. That's why I loved Sisi.

While Sisi was finishing up her pep talk, "Get Ready Ready" began to play by DJ Jubilee, and I ran to the grass underneath the tree to dance in the shade. It was a hot day, but we were still going to party like any other Sunday. I looked around at all of my family members and felt thankful despite my earlier encounter with Sky. Something was bothering her, and I couldn't understand what I did for the life of me. I shrugged my shoulders and decided to let it go for the time being. Sisi continued to play basketball, and I walked around and watched the scenery.

I grabbed a glass bottle of orange soda pop and headed to my favorite spot: the back of the house, atop Granddaddy's tractor. Sitting there, I listened to the birds chirping, the insects buzzing, and distant dogs barking. A smile spread across my face as I reveled in the power of nature, feeling at peace once more. I was almost born here. My mother nearly went into labor while overexerting herself, picking peanuts in the field, and a few hours later, she actually did. Granddaddy was livid. He admonished Mama all the way to the local hospital, commenting, "This hospital is only good for clipping ingrown toenails," as he sat in the waiting room alongside my father. When a nurse struggled to take my mother's blood pressure, Daddy decided to rush her to Jackson to give birth. They arrived just in time, and a few short hours later, I was born, even though they tried their best to delay my arrival by another two months. Being a preemie, I had arrived ahead of schedule. Subsequently, I spent nearly every summer here; it truly felt like my second home.

"Bunny Hop" by Da Entourage began to play, and I finally looked back towards the front of the house. Everyone seemed to be jolly and enjoying themselves. I descended from the tractor, ensuring I didn't rip my pants like I had done once or twice.

I moseyed back to the front of the house, taking a seat on the porch with my soda pop. Beside the front door, Mama, Auntie Royce, and Auntie Linda chatted, with Auntie Linda showing some pictures.

As Mama spoke, Auntie Royce turned to her with a scornful expression. "You hoe'd for those pictures!" Auntie Royce remarked smugly.

"Let's talk!" Mama retorted, shoving Auntie Royce backward over the threshold and onto the living room couch.

Before I knew it, they were going at it fiercely, fighting tooth and nail. I couldn't comprehend what sparked the altercation. Watching in disbelief, I felt an aversion to the violence, a sentiment I remember having even back then. The rest of the family rushed into the room to intervene.

Sunny, Auntie Royce's daughter, jumped in it and began pulling my mama's hair. I shook my head in sadness. My people were fighting over nothing while the family's patriarchy was actively dying. For once, he couldn't use his voice and stature to break it up. Grandpa was slowly wasting away before our eyes while his daughters were yet again at each other's throats. I didn't get the hatred. If I had a sister, I'd cherish her to infinity and beyond; however, God saw to that not being the case.

I stared on as the pair behaved like animals fighting about food. I wondered what the real story was there. Darren , my eldest brother, always speculated that the sisters' relationship was toxic and that Auntie Royce working for 'my father' seemed to worsen their relationship. I didn't know how true that was, but I did not want to find the truth.

Pussy Policy #10: Never allow your husband or boyfriend to work with or around your sisters.

It often ended in disaster. Many men take pleasure in sleeping with 'real sisters'. It's despicable, but who am I to judge? The fight was eventually broken up by Auntie Linda's new boyfriend, Brandon, who was a police officer. Auntie Royce and her family left shortly afterward. I looked at Grandpa after the commotion, and he seemed pale. Being light-skinned, as his father was white, he was the direct result of a relationship between a former slave and a slave-master. This lineage made him a product of what some called the Mississippi curse: to be owned and never to own, one of the great American atrocities. Yet, this history made Grandpa incredibly resilient and strong-willed. He didn't resemble his former self much these days.

After the fight, his expression was somber, as if he wanted to reach for his belt, but he was too frail to even unwrap it from his drastically slim waist. I gave him a melancholic smile from beside his untouched birthday cake. Even smiling seemed to be a struggle for him, but he looked down at me affectionately.

"My sweet pea..." he murmured, his gaze full of warmth.

I wrapped my arms around his waist, giving him a hug. He seemed like he needed it. As he patted my back, I held on tighter, knowing that moments like these were becoming increasingly scarce.

***

June 1, 2005
Jackson, Mississippi

Granddaddy passed away at one o'clock in the afternoon. He had waited for my grandmother to arrive before saying his final goodbye. She had been his only wife; though he had many companions afterward, he never married again. Despite everything, she still held a special place in his heart. He yearned to see her one last time before he took his final breath, and she obliged, making it to the hospice floor of the hospital around noon. By then, he had been holding on for hours, measuring each breath. The weight of the pain he had caused her over the years was evident in the deep regret that clouded his eyes. Perhaps the only thing more painful than rejection is regret. At that moment, words couldn't change the consequences of his life choices. As he lay on his deathbed, his final wish had been granted, which in itself was a gift.

"Well, I'm a widow now…" Grandma remarked, a hint of sorrow in her eyes.

"Mama, you're not a—" Auntie Sarah began to correct Grandma but was silenced by her eldest sister, Auntie Flo.

Technically, to be a widow, one had to have been married, but no one felt the need to shatter Grandma's perception at that moment. She was already in grief. In her heart, she was, and always would be, his wife.

"Well, as a widow, I guess I'll seek the company of other women my age who are widows, too," Grandmother declared, distancing herself from the rest of us in the hospital waiting room. I had never seen my mama cry so intensely. I was in a state of shock and confusion also. I wasn't sure what death truly meant, but from what I could discern, it brought nothing but heartbreak and anguish.

God help us all.

Chapter 5

LESSONS FROM THE REARING

"Being a parent does not come with a road map or a set of instructions, but it's still the greatest mystical journey known to man."
~Sovereign Jane Jenkins

February 10, 2008
Jackson, Mississippi

As Mr. Tony took care of the patrons and provided service for the people in the Verdin district, aka the ghetto of Jackson, Mississippi, I would watch people from a distance. The patrons would come and go in a regular pattern. They grabbed whatever knick-knacks they came for and left. My father would turn to me and laugh as if he knew all the secrets in the world to life. The Bible he owned sat underneath the register as a foundation of the business. That seemed to be his guiding force, but the question that always seemed to pop into my head was, 'Why did he have cycles of pure evil?' It was almost like he enjoyed making me, my mother, and my brother suffer between the good times. It was psychological abuse at its finest. How could a keen and successful man treat the people he 'loved' so indisputably wrong? He victimized us but then acted like the victim afterward. I realized that he might have read the Word, but the devil still influenced him. He didn't love money; he loved the things that money could buy, like my mother, for example. So, he objectified us because, in his mind, he owned us, but the truth was we never belonged to him. He flexed his power using his wallet. Money doesn't always make you better; it simply enhances who you are already.

As I daydreamed about becoming the next female president, a woman entered the store. She appeared ill, unkempt and carried an unpleasant odor. It felt as though she ushered in a suffocating wave of bad scent. My father glanced at me, his expression urging me to take note of this woman. She ambled in, her attire suggesting she had dressed hastily. After selecting a beer, a coke, and some cigarettes, she approached the counter to pay.

"Hey, Tony! How are you doing?" she greeted nonchalantly.

"Hey! Having a good day?" he responded. When she proffered a crumpled ten-dollar bill, he subtly indicated she should place it on the counter rather than handing it directly to him. She momentarily looked affronted but soon regained her composure. Her skin had a pallid, gray hue, and deep circles under her eyes hinted at prolonged exhaustion. Her hair was slicked back in a style reminiscent of a chicken. Though I was reluctant to label it a 'chicken head,' the description seemed apt. Sores surrounded her mouth, appearing as indistinct bumps, their color obscured by the protective clear glass between us. She looked fatigued, almost run down. Dressed in a white tank top and short cloth pants, her slender legs and frail stature suggested malnutrition. I found myself pondering her life story.

"Thanks, Tony," she grumbled as she walked out of the store.

"You see her?"

How could I miss her? I thought to myself.

"She was drugged at a party when she was a teenager. The men that were present gang-raped her and gave her HIV. It's now full-blown AIDS."

My eyes bucked in confusion. I was young, but my mother had taught me what rape was at the age of four. I was floored. She had a rough life based on her decisions and the circumstances around her life. Mr. Tony turned to me then with a serious, pondering look on his face.

"Don't let that be you," he said, watching her exit. He took the alcohol bottle and doused the ten-dollar bill with the solution, treating her as if she were a leper. I felt deep sympathy for her, imagining that she faced such treatment everywhere she went. She seemed to bore her lot with a deeper sorrow than any I had seen. A wave of sadness engulfed me, thinking of the daily pain she must've felt from being treated by the world as if she were worthless. I sat in silence, unable to find words. Mr. Tony continued to clean the ten-dollar bill, seemingly oblivious to her suffering. While he appeared desensitized to the world's pain, continuing as if nothing had happened, I was deeply affected. It was then that I established my very eleventh rule.

Pussy Policy 11: All it takes is one sexual encounter to alter the course of your life.

Statistics:

- According to HIV.GOV, 1.2 million Americans are HIV positive, while 13% unknowingly have it.
- According to Planned Parenthood, 1 in 6 Americans have genital herpes.
- Also according to Planned Parenthood, over half of Americans have oral herpes.
- According to CDC.GOV, 42.5 million Americans have been infected by the HPV virus, which is the most common STI.
- According to the Center for Disease control, new STDs have cost $16 billion dollars within the medical system in the United States.

I still remember that day like it was yesterday. It was one of those defining moments in my life where I created my boundaries and living standards. I usually played alone, and I explored the world by myself. No one would ever touch me without having an STD test and a condom, I thought to myself at such an impressionable age. Mr. Tony sugar-coated nothing, and for that, I was grateful. I needed that kind of truth because I was so gullible and curious because I was so young, not due to my lack of intelligence. He recognized that it was his job to give me those principles. He was hard on my brother and I for whatever reason. Of course, he was harder on me than my brother. It was the double standard that I couldn't escape in my household.

"Mr. Tony, when can I start going on dates?" I asked curiously. He blinked thoughtfully.

"When you're thirty," he said without hesitation. I blinked with my mouth wide open then.

He couldn't have been serious… But he let my brother go out of town for his dates during his teenage years.

As the seconds ticked by, I realized he was as serious as a heart attack. "Why thirty?" I complained. His face formed a smirk, but he never explained or hinted at the reason. He just looked at me with a peculiar expression, knowing that revealing the reason would clue me into the type of man he had been to my mother. My mother entered the store just then, and my father led me to the back. He handed me a newspaper, a displeased look evident on his face. He disapproved of me watching my Saturday morning cartoons. "What's wrong with Jimmy Neutron?" I pondered. Instead of letting me indulge in TV, he instructed me to analyze the newspaper, warning that he would quiz me on it later. It felt like pure torture for a child. "Janeka will be just fine as long as she doesn't let anyone trick her," I overheard my father tell my mother as I clutched the thin piece of paper.

I was confused. What exactly did he mean by that? He had no intention of explaining it then, so I realized I had to discover that for myself. What he meant was:

Tony's Policy:
No sex.
No four-course dinners.
No cleaning up.
No making a home.
No washing clothes.
No wife benefits.
Don't be a wife without a ring.
You get no benefits in the end.

Why was he always telling me what to do anyway? He wasn't my father...

Chapter 6

※

TAKING CHANCES

"Just like mistakes are meant to be made, prices are meant to be paid. Whatever you do, take a chance and find your way."
~**Sovereign Jane Jenkins**

Hattiesburg, Mississippi
October 21, 2017

Pussy Policy #12: Never assume anything; ask questions.

The night before race day swiftly approached, and I was beyond nervous. I hadn't seen Gia in nearly a decade. While I hoped that things hadn't changed too much between us over the past ten years, I recognized that change and growth are imperative parts of life's journey. We had been practically children in the fourth grade, and now, we were grown women. Things were different.

On my drive down to the Gulf Coast, I had to pee so badly that I stopped along the road and used a large McDonald's cup because the service station I had pulled up next to was closed. I couldn't help but laugh at myself for being in such a precarious situation, thinking things could be worse. I texted Gia, who informed me they were all out for dinner at a restaurant around the corner from the hotel, a place known for its wings. Heading that way, I arrived and took a moment to look in the mirror, sighing. I reassured myself that this could be a great experience. I had the chance to make new friends, reconnect with an old one, and improve my fitness. This was shaping up to be an awesome weekend! And it didn't disappoint.

I walked into the sparsely occupied restaurant, searching for a three-person table. It didn't take me long to find it. Gia and her boyfriend were facing me, while her best friend's back was turned my way. As I walked up the steps, Gia's and my eyes locked. It was like seeing a ghost. A whole decade had passed. She rose when she saw me, and as we embraced, it felt as though no time had passed at all. It was deeply heartening to reconnect; feelings of genuine affection from the past surged back, and I remembered why I was once so taken with her. It was her inner light, a light I recognized in myself. Some people exude an innocence and purity that makes it comforting to be around them. That's how this reconnection felt. In my humble opinion, Gia was the only woman I'd ever met whose beauty rivaled my own. I didn't feel insecure or see her as a competition. Deep down, I regarded her as a love I had never pursued. It's intriguing how the human mind works. At that moment, I was simply a virgin, a student, and an old friend from the past. Although I felt a proclamation of love rising within me, I tucked that sentiment away as I approached her.

"It's good to see you," I said.

"It's good to see you too," she said.

After embracing Gia, I turned to the table to meet the people I would spend the next forty-eight hours of my life with. There was Vince, her boyfriend. He was very attractive. Very tall and had great vibes.

"Hello, how are you?" I said while shaking his hand.

"Hey, I'm good. And you?" he said pleasantly with a smile.

Then I turned to Gia's best friend, expecting a flamboyant metrosexual male. He didn't appear to be homosexual. I didn't find him very attractive either, and I immediately thought to myself that it would be easy to brush him off. He simply wasn't what I was looking for. Granted, I wasn't perfect in the looks or body department. I was 50 pounds overweight and trying my best to get it off and present my best self to the world. I have struggled with my weight my entire life, which was an insecurity of mine. However, I knew I was a beautiful woman regardless, so I carried myself as an overweight college woman. My hair was worn because I expected to get it dirty at the race, but there he was with a darker skin tone, dreads that hadn't been tightened in a while, big eyes, big nose, big lips, and ironically had, teeth like mine. His voice was bounding yet musical, but I wasn't very attracted to him still. He was very skinny with a tiny frame, and I was pretty sure that I could pick him up and toss him around with one arm. I didn't try it, of course.

"Hello, how are you?" I said pleasantly.

He finally looked up from his phone, and I said, "Hey, Michael. Nice to meet you!"

We shook hands, and I took a seat next to Michael. We all chatted and laughed for about two hours. Gia and I caught up on what's next and laughed about the good ole days of the fourth grade. Michael paid his phone a lot of attention, looking at odd things, from centipedes to quirky nature videos on his phone. He seemed physically there but far away at the same time.

I thought to myself about how turned off I was, and Vince gave me a funny look while silently kicking Michael under the table. Michael finally looked up and began to engage more in the conversation.

"What's the deal with people today?" he asked as we both glanced at the news station playing in the restaurant. Although the news reports made it seem like madness and anarchy were taking over, we all knew they were exaggerating.

"I don't know, but I just live here," I said with a chuckle.

"Yeah, we all do at this point," he said thoughtfully.

"Are y'all excited about the race tomorrow?"

"Hell, yeah!" Michael said enthusiastically.

"I'm just ready to get across the finish line," said Gia.

"This should be good because I brought my Go-pro," said Vince.

"This is not nearly as difficult as a Spartan Race. I ran one a few weeks back with my brother and his girlfriend," Michael said, pulling up the pictures on his phone.

The Spartan Race appeared to be very challenging and damn well intimidating.

"Who wants to kill themselves to get over a finish line nearly?" I thought to myself.

"That's awesome! I can't believe you did that," I said, genuinely impressed. The kid seemed to have guts.

Michael chuckled with me, and soon after, both Gia and Vince excused themselves to the bathroom. I suspected it was a planned move to get me comfortable with the idea that we would be sharing a room for the next two nights. Regardless, I was prepared. I had my pepper spray in my night bag and a knife beside it, just in case. While my mother raised me to be a lady, she wasn't privy to the details of this adventure. She certainly didn't know about me sleeping in the same room as my old best friend's current best friend, who happened to be a guy. If she knew, she would have a fit. Being the youngest and the only girl of three siblings, I was raised as a conservative young lady by my mother.

"Where are you from?" he asked.

"Jackson, Mississippi," I said

"Me too."

"Are your parents still there?"

"Yes," I said, they live on the city's outskirts.

Little did we know, we lived just thirteen minutes apart from each other, attending two completely different high schools. We found common ground and shared similar interests, notably the fact that we were both set to graduate from college the following May. Talking to him was both exciting and refreshing. He neither completely irked my nerves nor turned me off, which was a positive sign. I tried not to stare, but being analytical, I couldn't help but memorize every feature, from the bridge of his nose to the slight indentation on his forehead, even the wrinkle in his nose when certain topics arose. Our rapport surprised me, especially considering I identified as asexual and typically had no strong feelings for the opposite sex, a sentiment largely influenced by my upbringing. My dad had always said I couldn't date until I was 30. Now that I'm approaching that age, I completely understand his rationale. I plan to give my daughter the same advice.

I digress. Eventually, Gia and Vince returned to the table, and our conversation continued. I didn't order anything; my stomach was in knots, partly due to the upcoming race and this unexpected gathering. Gia handed me the room key while I electronically transferred the funds for the room to Michael. They all settled their food bills. When Michael finally stood up beside me, I hadn't realized how much he towered over me. At 6 foot 4 inches, compared to my 5 foot 4 inches, I suddenly recognized that I was the shortest in the group. A thought crossed my mind that this might be a mistake: they could leave me in the dust during the run. However, that didn't mean I was about to concede defeat before the race even began. I was ready to take on the challenge. Just not at that exact moment since I was exhausted and needed some rest. The race was scheduled to start at 8:00 a.m., meaning we'd all need to rise early to arrive on time.

We made our way back to the hotel. Michael rode with Gia and Vince while I drove alone. Once we arrived, I carried my duffle bag up to the room where Michael was already sitting on the bed, engrossed in his phone. I initiated a casual conversation to keep the atmosphere light, given that he didn't seem to be heading to sleep anytime soon. We chatted for a good 30 minutes, finding common ground in our shared love for food, physical activity, trying new things, and exploring new places. By that time, I had traveled to more destinations than he had, even though he was two years older than me. He hadn't even purchased his passport yet. I had been to Spain, Italy, Mexico, Jamaica, and various parts of the U.S. In contrast, his only trip outside his usual environment was to Florida for a modeling opportunity as a young adult. While he was working, the rest of his family enjoyed a vacation.

I quickly slipped into my night clothes in the bathroom and prepared for bed. I felt comfortable around him, so I only wore my nightdress and no underwear. Looking back, maybe I was being provocative and promiscuous. In my defense, this was how I slept every night, honestly. We continued to ramble into the night about silly, mundane things into the early morning, and we both eventually fell asleep around 4:00 a.m., only to be up at 07:00 a.m. to make it to the race around 08:00 a.m. The bed was so uncomfortable I don't think we even slept; it was more akin to drifting with our eyes closed.

Pussy Policy#13: Never tease a man and put yourself in a vulnerable situation with him.

Now, looking back, I knew I was playing with fire. Being in my nightgown with no panties on in the same room with a straight, heterosexual male was not a good idea. It went against all my self-imposed and reared principles, yet there I was.

Chapter 7

DANGLING THE FRUIT

"Even though the forbidden fruit is sweet, the vines are still sharp."
~Sovereign Jane Jenkins

Gulfport, Mississippi
October 21, 2017

On race day, we were slow to rise. Getting Michael out of bed was an act of Congress; he slept so hard. I slept lightly. He snored. I didn't. I wrote myself a mental note to grab some earplugs from the store for the following night. I was excited! I refused to be late. It was my first race and another step towards my fitness journey. I was like a ball of energy. Gia and Vince met us in the lobby. We didn't have time to grab breakfast, so we would run the 5k- all 3.1 miles- on an empty stomach. Talk about an upset stomach. It was a good time, however. We ended up completing the run in an hour. We went down a slide at the end that led into a pool of mud water; luckily, I could swim. Somebody kicked Gia in the head at the bottom of the pool of muck. I laughed because I was ahead of them most of the run. They were all tall, but ultimately, running is about stamina. What beats stamina and energy? Not much, and I had both; I had already lost thirty pounds by then on my fitness journey, which allowed me to persist even when my knees were hurting, my back was aching, and my nipples were burning from the bra chafing.

We all crossed the finish line, and I caught up with Miss E, my personal trainer, to get a group picture. They finished the race in 30 minutes, as I had expected. They passed us at some point during the race, and all I could do was wave because my body refused to keep up physically. Miss E ran right past us with her shoes off; the extremist she was, even the shoes themselves refused to stay on. I laughed at the thought as she ran by. I was exhausted, muddy, and happy all at the same time, but that didn't stop me from grabbing a beer and doing my victory dance next to the liquor station and music once it was all over. Unfortunately, I had forgotten my shoes in my dorm room, so I had to walk around without shoes on my feet in the dirt. Michael took a look at my feet and took his shoes off of his feet. He handed me his shoes.

"Put these shoes on," he said.

"Really," I said.

"Yeah, you don't need to walk around here without shoes on."

"Thank you!" I said in surprise.

No one had ever shown me that kind of kindness that wasn't close to me or related to me. I was genuinely appreciative of the gesture.

"No problem." He said, handing them to me. He walked around in his socks while we grabbed the complimentary drinks from the bar. I got to cross a goal off my list; I was ecstatic. In celebration, I danced to Beyoncé, Shakira, Donna Summer, Justin Bieber, Tim McGraw, and Faith Hill for a good thirty minutes or so. Everyone was finally ready to eat, so we wrapped up the dancing and festivities to go eat. Michael and I walked ahead to the car while Gia and Vince stayed behind to use the porta-potty. We decided to be mischievous together and move the car from its original position. They came out and walked our way, and we jumped out of the car so that they would search for it for a few minutes. We laughed silently to ourselves at the sheer childish nature of the actions. Vince and Gia walked our way.

We walked away from the car and acted like we were still searching for it.

"Babe, I could've sworn it was right here," we heard Vince say while holding his Go-pro.

"It was right here," she said in a worried voice.

She had rented the car using her account, so it was only a matter of time before she freaked out.

We walked up behind them laughing, unable to hold in the humor.

They turned around and looked at us. I guess our faces gave it away.

"Guys, have y'all seen the car?"

"It's over there," Michael pointed out as we both snickered. We all decided on a seafood place nearby, so we headed to a restaurant by the bay of the Gulf Coast. It was a beautiful day. It was warm, open, and not pressured. It had a positive and fresh energy. I was happy to be a part of the group that day. I'm glad to have stepped out on a leap of faith.

Pussy Policy #14: Never shoot your shot at a man. He needs to be able to shoot on his own; that's the confidence that will sustain his pursuit of the relationship.

***

On the way to the restaurant, Vince drove while Michael and I sat quietly in the backseat, recovering from our earlier adventure through the forest and mud tunnels. I playfully hit him on the arm, and he looked at me, returning the gesture. I knew I was playing with fire, something I occasionally did. But it went deeper than that. That simple gesture opened the door to more than I had bargained for. Now, I was the prey, and he was the hunter. This seemingly innocent action made me vulnerable in ways I hadn't anticipated. At the restaurant, Michael sat to my left, Gia to my right, and Vince directly in front of me. Watching the affectionate couple was awkward since I had never expressed or felt such affection with anyone. Michael seemed lost in thought, perhaps wrestling with his own internal battles.

After eating, I stepped outside to sit on the dock, taking in the view of the sea. Michael joined me, both of us feeling somewhat out of place around the enamored pair. He busied himself on his phone while I took photos for keepsakes. At one point, our eyes met, but he quickly looked away. With a smile, I brushed off the brief moment of tension. After Gia and Vince settled their bill, we headed back to the hotel.

Once in our room, Michael kindly offered me the first turn in the shower. Ridding my skin of the day's dirt, grime, and red mud felt heavenly. Once clean, we both took a much-needed siesta, a Spanish tradition of a midday nap to rejuvenate one's spirit. While he showered, he played music. Though I would have preferred silence, I was too exhausted to voice any objection. I managed to drift off, waking later in the afternoon feeling refreshed. He, however, was sound asleep beside me. Waking him was always a challenge. He could probably sleep through an apocalypse without a care, a trait I envied since I've never been able to do the same.

"How did you sleep?" he asked.

"Well," I said, yawning and sitting under the covers with my hair wet and wrapped in a towel.

"Awesome! Gia just asked if we were down for food and shopping. You feel like going out?"

"Yeah, that sounds good," I said while stretching and preparing to get dressed.

"Nice nightgown," he said with a laugh.

"Nice slob mark," I said, pointing to his face, holding back a boisterous laugh as he ran into the bathroom in embarrassment. I noticed he had dry lips. I thought to myself how I had the perfect solution to that plight.

We were both dressed and ready for our outing in less than an hour. We met Gia and Vince in the lobby after stopping at the front desk to grab some complementary chocolate chip cookies. What can I say? I love the term "gratis." Living in Spain for six weeks one summer had certainly been beneficial.

"Hey, guys! Y'all ready?" Gia asked.

"Of course!" I responded with a smile. I felt genuinely happy and excited to be around people who didn't make me self-conscious about my weight. I was truly myself. And although I had feelings for Gia, I knew that nothing would happen between us. I respected Vince and was starting to warm up to Michael. He had a quirky charm, but I kept thinking he wasn't quite my type. I mean, my one hundred ninety-pound frame could probably overpower his one hundred and sixty-pound frame on a bad day. But maybe, just maybe, it would be worth it.

We found ourselves at an outlet store, walking around and sharing laughs. The hotel had a jacuzzi, and we were all eager to use it. The only issue was that I didn't have a bathing suit. Gia looked at me with a playful smirk.

"No bathing suit, no problem!" she declared, heading towards a store that seemed to carry swimwear. I eyed the store skeptically; it didn't even look like they carried plus sizes. But I thought, what the hell, might as well give it a shot.

Gia picked out a low-cut, burgundy number. I was hesitant, but it was on the clearance rack, so I figured, why not? I bought it. She looked satisfied, and so did I. Meanwhile, the guys were somewhere in the store, messing around and laughing.

"You fit in with our trio perfectly, Neka," Gia commented as we shopped. I was half-listening; I tend not to put too much stock in words alone. Actions speak louder. Is this genuine affection?

Later, we took a photo to send to Amber, the third member of our childhood trio. It felt almost ironic that I'd initially thought this reunion was a bad idea. Maybe this was meant to be. Or was it?

I made sure to grab my earplugs before walking out of the store; I had every intention of getting a good night's rest. I winked at Michael because he looked offended as I picked up the earbuds. 'He'll be alright!' I thought to myself while laughing aloud.

"What do you need those for?"

"To sleep."

"Are you trying to say I snore or something?"

"I'm not trying to say anything… Except you do!" I said with a smirk.

"Whatever," he laughed good-naturedly.

I smiled at the lovely couple as they were talking and flirting.

Michael and I passed by this guy who happened to be balding with dreads.

"Man, at some point, you gotta let it go," he said, staring at the man's head.

"Stop!" I said, stifling a hard laugh and trying my best not to look back. I failed miserably.

We both stood there laughing, and eventually, it turned into light-hearted flirting.

We grabbed some more food and headed back to the hotel. We decided to meet in twenty minutes at the jacuzzi. That was the going plan for the evening after we jumped into our bathing suits. Our bodies were aching from the rigorous run, which sounded marvelous in theory. One problem arose; I put on the bathing suit, and I was practically naked or next to it. My breasts were nearly spilling out of the bathing suit. And my rear end. I said to myself, this was just great! I had nothing else to wear, so I lacked options and time. I put it on with ambivalence and walked out with a towel around my waist because, as fate would have it, I had also neglected to shave down below. "Oh, well," I thought. It's inconsequential. No one's going down there. Michael looked up from his phone and averted his eyes when I came into view. I thought, well, at least he's not cracking jokes at this silly ordeal.

"Gia set me up," I said under my breath, which he didn't hear, thank heavens.

"Are you ready?"

"Yep!"

Before we made our way down to the pool, we knocked on Gia and Vince's door. Thinking they might already be downstairs—since no one answered—we headed down. To our surprise, both Gia and Vince were absent. At that moment, I realized it might be a setup.

"Gia wouldn't set me up," Michael commented, laughing as he sat against the pool wall. I blinked and stared at him, unamused. The humor eventually drained from his face as an hour passed, and we found ourselves still sitting alone in the jacuzzi.

"You know they aren't coming, right?" I finally remarked with a smirk.

"Yeah," he replied, positioning himself at the far end of the hot tub, maintaining a safe distance. The risqué design of the bathing suit meant that my chest was prominently on display, but at least I felt somewhat comfortable. "They probably fell asleep."

"Probably," I agreed, diverting my gaze from him for a moment. "At least it's warm in here."

Out of pure curiosity, I asked, "Are you a virgin?"

"No, I'm not." His response caught me off guard. He had the air of someone who might be, not because of his appearance but due to his demeanor. He struck me as a bit nerdy. Yet, as I soon realized, whether nerdy or not, he was still very much a man and that fact took precedence over all else.

"Why do you ask?" he said, moving closer to me. That made me extremely nervous as my heart rate sped up.

"It's just a question."

"Do you LOOK like a virgin?"

"I'll take that as a rhetorical question."

"It wasn't."

"I'm a virgin," I said confidently because I had considered myself asexual for so long.

"How old are you again?"

"Twenty-two."

"Twenty-two, and you're a virgin? Have you been under a rock?"

"What?" I said, laughing at him.

"I'm just saying. Twenty-two years and nothing? Why?"

"Long story short, I was raised with older brothers and a semi-strict mother."

"Ooh."

"Yep."

"So, no oral sex?"

"Nope."

"What about fingering?"

"Absolutely not for pleasure. Just by the gynecologist." He belly laughed, but I was serious.

"Why are you waiting?"

"My parents said all it takes is one time to catch a life-altering STD. So, I chose to wait. My faith also said wait. I'm Christian."

"Me, too. Well, me and my dad are, but my mom's a Jew.."

" How did that happen?"

"Long story short, that's how my mom grieved her mother's death. So, she never skips a Saturday. Even when she's nearly sick and near death, she's making it to the temple."

"Interesting," I said, looking away and wondering what could happen to me that would cause me to change my faith.

"So, would you like oral?"

"Huh," I said in confusion.

"Would you like for me to give you oral sex?"

I was in shock. No one had ever in this lifetime asked me a question like that.

"You didn't answer the question," he said, inching closer.

I was rendered speechless. It felt as though my mouth was stuffed with cotton, and my head tilted slightly to the right as if trying to make sense of his proposal.

"I'll give you head," he continued.

"I got it. But why?" I asked.

"Why what?"

"Why would you offer that?"

He was only a few inches away from me. I stood up from the jacuzzi to put some distance between us and quell the rising tension. He looked up at me, waiting for a reply, but I had none.

"I dare you to jump into the pool," I challenged, walking around the pool, nonchalantly flaunting my exposed figure. Before I had even done a full lap, he leaped out of the jacuzzi and into the pool.

"Now it's your turn," he said with a mischievous grin.

"Oh no," I thought to myself, realizing the predicament I'd landed in. Taking a deep breath, I dove into the pool from the opposite end. He laughed as I shrieked from the cold, immediately leaping out and rushing back to the warmth of the jacuzzi. He trailed behind me, amused by my attempts to warm up.

"I'll keep you warm," he whispered, his arms enveloping me and hands finding my thighs. Suddenly, the jacuzzi's warmth felt overwhelming. Before I could react, he disappeared beneath the water, drawing closer to me. I panicked, considering escaping.

Emerging for air, he swiftly caught me before I could flee. "Hey," he murmured, "just relax." But I couldn't. Before I could voice my discomfort, he kissed me deeply and intensely. My thoughts were consumed by the potential audience watching from the hotel windows above. Pushing him away, I tried to regain my composure.

"Calm down," I urged, my voice shaky.

"Just oral. I was in a committed relationship until recently. It's been months since we broke up. I'm ready to move on. So, I'm asking you directly: Do you want oral?" he pressed.

Pussy Policy #15: Never start a relationship off sexually. It'll fade with time because it's simply surface-level lust, nothing more—no sustenance of note.

I swallowed, unsure of how to respond. He chuckled and drew me into another kiss. My thoughts raced: 'Why now? Why him? What am I doing?' This was all uncharted territory for me. Keen to avoid seeming desperate or promiscuous, I chose silence. Mistaking my silence for consent, he deepened the kiss. I could feel the pressure of his desire against me. My heart raced, and I pulled away.

"I wonder what Gia and Vince are up to?" I said, trying to divert the topic. Climbing out of the jacuzzi, I wrapped a towel around me to shield myself and began walking towards the hotel entrance. He was quick to follow, reaching me just as I pressed the elevator button. Silent tension enveloped us during the ascent to the 5th floor. I hoped and prayed that Gia and Vince would be awake, offering a reprieve from the sexual attraction I felt brewing within.

No such luck. No one came to the door as I knocked patiently once more while trying to distract myself from the raging hormones that I was experiencing. I felt like a teenager again, but I was confused because I wasn't initially attracted to him. There I was, looking like prey to the predator, but the unfortunate part was I wanted it. I wanted to know what it was like to have an orgasm finally. What was that special feeling like?

That night, I found out exactly what it was like. He ate me for what felt like a good three hours off and on from touching, kissing, hugging, and all the things I've always wondered about happened that night, except intercourse.

Pussy Policy #16: Never drop your guard prematurely.

I dropped my guard prematurely because the head was just that good: my head was gone after that.

Chapter 8

FALLING IN LOVE

*"Falling could mean hitting the ground.
I'd rather float to nirvana;
Even though nirvana is a realm of lust.
But the final destination could lead to love."*
~Sovereign Jane Jenkins

Gulfport, Mississippi
October 22, 2017

The next morning came soon enough. I woke up to him lying to my right. I felt like a new woman, all open and free. It was the dopamine hitting my pleasure center—a false high. Although I gave him a taste of my body, I wasn't ready to give him my full heart. So, I lay there and stared at him until the morning sun disturbed his slumber.

"Hey," he said sleepily.

"Hey," I said calmly, laying beside him.

"Are you satisfied?" he said.

I had no idea what that meant. I didn't know what else it was supposed to feel like. The question in my eyes let him know that I did not orgasm. So, he flipped me onto my back and tried it again before it was time to check out. He was unsuccessful. I felt bad because maybe it was me. Maybe I was broken. There could have been a disconnect between my body and my mind, just like there seemed to be a disconnect in my sexuality occasionally. I seemed to fall in love with women, but my body craved men. It was a weird experience, but I had to be patient with myself because I did not know what to expect regarding love, sex, and relationships. It was a new world that I could not wait to explore, and that worried him.

"Are you ok?"

"Yes, why do you ask?"

"Because of that look on your face."

I was at a loss for words. It was intimate. The whole experience was sweet, but I wasn't sure what he expected from me. I shrugged my shoulders and glanced toward my phone when it vibrated. It was a text from Gia.

"Speak of the devil. Well, well, well. I guess they're still alive," I remarked with a smirk.

His phone buzzed as well. It was her text, informing us we had to check out in thirty minutes. I winked at him as I lay beside him, our bare bodies wrapped in a shared warmth. Unexpectedly, she video-called him, and of course, he answered, lying in my bed. As he kept the camera on himself and then panned over to me, I'm sure my face turned beet red. Nevertheless, I remained in bed – it was my territory, after all.

"Hey, Gia!" I greeted.

"Hey, Neka! I'm glad you two are up. I'll meet you both downstairs in a few minutes, okay?"

She ended the call, and I turned to Michael. He shrugged; I did the same. We both hurriedly got dressed. His lips, dry from our extensive nighttime and early morning escapades, needed attention. So, I handed him my secret weapon, one he'd come to appreciate for years after: Vaseline's lip therapy balm. It's the best remedy for chapped lips, and I never leave home without it.

Now, back to our regularly scheduled program.

We met up with Gia and Vince downstairs in the hotel lobby once again for breakfast, and they both had silly grins on their faces. I felt hot-faced because the cat was out of the bag. I was a little slut, but not really, because I didn't go all the way. So, I was technically a curious soul. Rather, I was simply a young woman searching for herself in the world.

"What happened to you guys last night? We knocked on your door and everything," I asked half-heartedly.

"Sorry, girl. Well, we 'got it in' and fell asleep," Gia said without a hint of regret. "So... the jacuzzi was never the plan?" She laughed and headed to our table, taking a seat. The rest of us followed suit. Vince wore a knowing smirk. I sat quietly, deliberately avoiding making eye contact with Michael. At some point over the weekend, I acquired his number. Now, I figured, it was a matter of waiting for his call. "How did y'all sleep?" Vince asked, a hint of mischief in his voice, just as our food arrived. Gia tried to suppress her grin as she sipped her coffee. "I slept great," I responded cheerfully, quickly diverting my attention to my toast to sidestep the growing awkwardness. My gaze shifted to Michael. Nervousness crept in. Initially, I hadn't been attracted to him. I couldn't envision a future with him. It might sound vain, but in a world where appearances often matter, I prided myself on my looks – at least from the neck up. He was average-looking, skinny, and tall with dreads. I chastised myself for such thoughts, yet, that was my unfiltered truth.

"So, are y'all planning to go out on a date?" Gia probed expectantly. In my head, this was a one-night-stand type of deal. Perhaps we could be friends, but nothing more.

"Because I'm thinking of giving Michael your number," Gia added as if reading my mind. "He already has it," I mentioned, which elicited a giddy squeal from her. Finally, I allowed myself a brief glance in Michael's direction. He was giving Gia a broad, Cheshire-cat grin. It was endearing, but I remained skeptical about our potential future. The overarching question loomed: what was the point? "Y'all make such a cute pair," Gia commented. Internally, I snarkily thought: I'm the cute one. I mentally chided myself for such thoughts. Despite my reservations, I committed to one date. After all, what was the worst that could happen?

As breakfast concluded and we all got ready to depart, I offered Michael a brief hug and wished him, Gia, and Vince, a safe journey back to the city. I set off for my college campus, roughly an hour's drive away, to prep for an upcoming nursing exam. Exhausted from the weekend's activities, I climbed into bed without sending Michael a message. Both of us, I sensed, needed time to reflect. Eventually, sleep enveloped me, offering a peaceful escape.

I swam playfully along the edge of the pool, little floaties on my arms. My mom sat by the steps, chatting with one of our neighbors, Wade. Engrossed in her conversation, she wasn't watching me. Seizing the moment, I removed my floaties; I wanted to swim unaided, like a fish, to impress my momma. I placed the floaties on the concrete slab near the filter and stood up. The water reached my shoulders. Chayne was out of sight, probably running around with the white boys from the apartment complex: Mikey, Spencer, and Jeff. They were fun, but I preferred the pool.

Venturing deeper, I soon found only my head above water. I attempted to swim, jumping and kicking, but my five-year-old frame sank. Trying to emulate my mom's backstroke, I felt I was just splashing around before sinking again. I panicked as I tried standing and realized the current had carried me closer to the deep end. As my feet couldn't touch the ground and my head submerged, I tried doggy paddling. Exhaustion set in quickly, and holding my breath wasn't my strength.

I didn't want to alert my mom, knowing she'd be upset about the floaties. I jumped, hoping to call out to her, but water choked my cries. Through the stinging water, I could see her chatting with Wade, oblivious to my plight. Multiple attempts to shout yielded the same results. My stomach hurt from swallowing water. I was just four years old. A bleak realization settled in: I might drown. I wouldn't get to hear my favorite songs or see my mom in her blue house dress anymore. As darkness threatened to engulf me, I prayed one more time.

Suddenly, her maternal instincts kicked in. Her gaze scanned the pool and locked onto mine just as I submerged again. The raw terror on her face was evident as she shouted, "Janeka!" That frantic tone was unfamiliar. Hearing her voice gave me a momentary boost, and I tried to cry out once more underwater. By now, tears mixed with the chlorinated water. My body felt unnaturally cold and heavy, especially given that I was underweight for my age. Just when I thought I'd succumb, strong arms pulled me out.

Breathing fresh air, I cried loudly. "Janeka!" my mom yelled, holding me close. She moved to the pool's edge and lifted me out. I burped up water between sobs. Holding me close, she slapped my back to expel more water, drawing the attention of the surrounding neighbors. Wrapped in a beach towel, she admonished, "Janeka, don't you ever do that again!" Tears filled her eyes. Wade, looking concerned, asked, "Is she okay?"

I jolted awake. Why was I dreaming about that memory? I looked around the room. I was safely in my dorm, tucked into my twin-sized bed. My heart was racing. That's weird because I never, ever dream. Why was it a childhood experience dream? I remember that day clearly. I had floated too far off in the pool, and thank heavens, Mama saw me at the last second and screamed my name. That was the only thing I heard as I went underwater once again. She saved me by pulling me out of the water that day. I sighed as I got up out of bed to pee. I sat on the toilet in silence. Why was that memory resurfacing now? Was it because of what I did with Michael in the jacuzzi? Was that a warning sign? I didn't know, but I promptly returned to bed because I had to attend class the next morning. I slept peacefully for the rest of the night.

***

The following night…

I texted Gia and Michael back and forth, gathering information to determine whether he was a good person and might be a good match for me.

Gia said, "He'll love you from your head to your toes. Just give him a chance. He got out of a relationship three months ago, and it was a horror show. She couldn't stand me, and the feeling was mutual."

I listened as she continued praising Michael, yet I remained hesitant. I was single, young, and free, with no rush to commit to anyone. However, I considered maybe giving him a chance.

Interrupting her mid-ramble, I asked, "Why didn't you choose him?"

"What do you mean?"

"Why did you choose to date Vince instead of Michael?"

"Michael was in a committed relationship at the time, and Vince and I started off just having fun. But when he wanted more, I told him, 'Give me a few days to sort out my past.'"

That piqued my interest. She found her husband while merely seeking fun. It's not always so fortunate. Often, women become 'years of fun' until the man finds 'the one' and leaves the former behind—selfishness epitomized.

"They dated for five years," Gia added. That statement made me sit up. Five years is a long commitment to simply let go.

"Is it really over between them?" I inquired, seeking clarity.

"Yes. He made it clear that the chapter is closed."

"Good to know because I'm still a virgin, and I'm not in a hurry to change that."

Gia, taken aback, exclaimed, "What!"

"I'm conservative about intimacy. I don't easily allow someone to get close physically. The idea of such closeness is unfamiliar and uncomfortable to me," I confessed.

"I respect that. It's commendable. What made you wait?"

I responded, "The better question is, why not wait? There's more to life than physical intimacy."

"Fair enough."

I've always been self-aware, deliberately choosing a path different from many of my peers. While others were experiencing first-time intimacies, I was at home watching TV, reading books, or exploring the woods. My parents drilled into me a singular warning: just once, ONE TIME, is all it takes to catch an incurable STD. That alone deterred me. I embraced a lifestyle that is vagina-conscious and vagina-safe. The risks tied to multiple partners aren't for me. I would've made different choices long ago if I desired that kind of trouble.

Pussy Policy # 17: Keep your legs closed, your eyes open, and your heart out of the equation until a man has proven himself.

"Hey girl, Michael's calling. I'll call you back," I said, ending the call before she could respond. Even though it had only been a day, I felt a pull towards him. That's the nature of soul ties; they pull you in effortlessly, much like quicksand, yet are incredibly challenging to break free from. I sighed, recognizing the burgeoning feelings. Was it love, or perhaps just the enchanting idea of it?

"Hey, I just got off the phone with Gia," I shared with enthusiasm.

"Hey, babe... I mean, Janeka."

The term of endearment caught me off guard. How did we get to this point so quickly? Our conversations seemed to stretch on endlessly, only ending when sleep took over. Finally, I voiced the question that had been nagging at me.

"Are you really over your ex?" I asked bluntly.

"If I weren't, I wouldn't be talking to you."

"Perhaps you're just looking for a rebound."

"I'm not. I'm over her."

"Alright. I'd like to meet her."

"Okay, I'll ask her," he replied, not hesitating.

"Good," I said, smirking. I was curious—whether it was the potential drama or a genuine interest in gauging his ex's feelings towards him. Regardless, I was ready to walk away if I sensed any lingering attachments. I didn't believe in wasting time, energy, or giving my all without reciprocity. My mother always advised letting a man prove himself before getting intimate. I had already bypassed that advice. I couldn't afford to compromise any further. They say love can make a fool of you, but actions reveal more than words.

The more time I spent with Michael, the deeper I found myself entangled in his world, often without even realizing it. His presence became a need; I yearned for his voice, his time, and his every thought. It's fascinating how emotions can be so consuming. Slowly, his influence began to seep into my core. As much as I resisted, I found myself bending my own rules for him.

Pussy Policy #18: Never fall in love; walk in love while he caresses your mind with his personality, temperament, speech, character, and, most importantly, his actions.

"Will you be my Girlfriend?" he asked over the phone while I sat at my dorm room desk.

Pussy Policy #19: If he doesn't make you his girlfriend within four months of dating, and you're dating intentionally, pull back and talk to someone else or focus on yourself.

"No," I said without hesitation. I heard the disappointment in his voice.

"Why not?"

"I don't know you."

"You're getting to know me."

"Tomato-Tamato."

"What?"

"Nothing. I'm not ready for a committed relationship," I said with certainty. There were too many variables that weren't locked in for me.

"Love is a gamble, Janeka."

"I'm not the gambling type, Michael."

"Then, when will you be?"

"I don't know…" I said, reflecting on my childhood. The traumatic events from my past weighed heavily on me. I yearned for tranquility in my adult life—nothing more. After working so hard, I refused to remain mired in misery. This drive is why I excelled in school; I understood that knowledge was the ticket to liberation. It always had been, and it always would be.

Having grown up in a single-parent home, Michael couldn't grasp these principles. He couldn't comprehend the profound hurt of parental rejection that made me wary of every man who entered my life. That emotional pain was something I had been grappling with for twenty-two long years. No, Michael couldn't fathom it, and I wasn't eager to enlighten him. It was my journey, my personal narrative.

As our conversation progressed, I could feel my energy waning, sapped by the demands of nursing school, this newfound connection, academic readings, and evolving friendship with Gia. I came to a realization: Michael and I would remain just friends. I had made peace with that conclusion. Even without personally experiencing heartbreak, I respected relationships. Observing its effects on my mother, who became bitter and harsh, solidified my stance. I didn't want her past to become my future. Though nursing school brought its stresses, overall, I was content. I was on my path to realizing my aspirations—first becoming a nurse and, eventually, a travel nurse.

Life was progressing, and that's what I needed. Not more people around me who would make me miserable. But, again, what do I know? I'm just living the life the good lord gave me.

"Please, be my girlfriend?" he said.

"Nope. How do I know that you are over your ex?"

"Because I'm telling you that that's my past, and you're my future."

"Good answer, and we'll see," I said with a solid resolve.

"Why did you choose me that night?" he asked.

"What do you mean?" I asked, confused.

"I know I'm not the 'first' choice or the 'go to' man in a group of people," he said.

"Why did I choose you? I didn't, Gia did," I laughed.

He went silent and appeared sad. I realized that he was looking for reassurance and an ego boost. I obliged him after letting him sweat for a few minutes.

" I chose you because you're a giving person. You gave me your shoes," I said honestly.

"I understand. I was just being a good Samaritan."

"Well, the act earned you major brownie points that you earned on your own."

"I don't know if I can do it again…"

"What do you mean?"

"You're with me because of Gia's testimony. I'm just saying I would have liked to have earned you with my own efforts. I didn't really EARN you."

"Well, keep proving yourself because it's not set in stone. Time will tell if it's meant to be," I said, giving him my honest point of view.

"Ok," he said, realizing I wouldn't spoon-feed him or stroke his ego.

"Do you have any quirks or pet peeves?" I said suddenly to change the conversation.

"Not really…I just don't brush my teeth at night because I prefer to do it once I wake up in the morning," he said.

My stomach dropped because that explained why his breath was hot in the morning once I woke up.

"Ew…No! You will have to work on that because sometimes your breath is…" I held back on the description, trying not to hurt his feelings.

"My ex didn't either; she would get these bumps on her tongue and pop them with her teeth."

"Ew. I don't need to know any of that. She's nasty, and my nose would appreciate it if you worked on your own personal hygiene."

"Ok…" he said, getting defensive, but I didn't care because I was serious. My nose couldn't take too many more insults.

"I'M JUST SAYING…I'm not trying to be funny or upset you," I said matter of fact.

"Well, I did just get through eating you out that morning that we woke up…' he said, suggesting that was the reason why his breath was rank.

"LOL. Don't even try it. It smelled the same the previous morning, too." I laughed, appalled that he was even suggesting that *my* coochie had his breath tart.

"Well, good night," he said, wanting to end the conversation before he said something offensive to me.

"Good night, Michael," I said calmly.

Chapter 9

TRUE COLORS

"The representation of oneself is not always reality because it's rooted in fantasy, but fantasy can not survive in the same realm as reality, Because both together equals a fallacy."
~Sovereign Jane Jenkins

Jackson, Mississippi
November 15, 2017

Everything isn't what it seems. What appears on the surface isn't always what's underneath. That's the lesson I learned with Gia. As time passed, her true colors began to surface and spill over the facade of genuineness. It was both slowly grating on my nerves and breaking my heart.

"Why did you bring her?" The text from Gia to Michael's phone chimed after we visited her together as a small outing.

I was taken aback by her apparent offense at Michael bringing me to her house. The situation felt peculiar. Then it dawned on me: her intense reaction stemmed from the perceived loss of her best friend or at least the time they once spent together. Because of our relationship, he was no longer as available to her as he used to be. After his breakup, she had become his emotional pillar. They hung out incessantly: he visited her often, spent his free hours with her outside of class, texted and called her continuously, and even stayed over at her place on occasions when he had consumed too much alcohol. Their dynamic had shifted dramatically, and rather than confronting the issue head-on, she vented her frustrations on him. Their bond felt more like that of siblings than mere best friends.

A realization hit me about the complications that arise when dating a man with a close female friend. Some argue that men and women can't maintain a platonic relationship. All I knew was that I was observant. I was watching closely, and I hoped they recognized that. They probably did. It's part and parcel of such dynamics. Any inklings of discomfort would be my cue to exit. By nature, I had always been one to flee. My profound fear of getting hurt dominated my feelings, especially considering our shared history. Now, I understand that our past didn't shield us from potential problems; this was merely the tip of the iceberg.

It was the red flags before the hard stop sign. I should have taken my heed, but I didn't.

"I brought her because I didn't realize it would be an issue."

"Well, you could have at least asked if I was ok with the company," Gia messaged.

"Am I considered 'company' now?" I mused internally. Though I've always been an empathetic individual—often referred to as 'Miss Too Understanding'—her logic baffled me. It was she who had introduced me to Michael and sung his praises, encouraging me to give him a chance with the zeal of a songbird. I had obliged, and this was the outcome. The situation was puzzling then, but everything became clear later on. She was trying to provoke a reaction, pushing buttons to draw attention. The consistent pettiness grew wearisome. I hadn't wronged her, nor did I feel any urge to, yet the unnecessary confrontations persisted.

"I apologize. Next time, I'll ask for permission. It won't happen again," he texted.

I blinked in disbelief. What! Seriously. I'm at a loss for words. It was like he was bowing down to his 'big sister,' but he was older than her. Crazy shit, I know. I felt like I was in the twilight zone. I leaned back in my car seat and pondered the entire interaction. This definitely had my attention. I was all eyes and ears.

I looked at Michael from the passenger seat of his old Audi in confusion.

"What was all that about?"

"I don't know," he said, eyebrows furrowed. "Let's just drop it."

"My mother always said you'll have few real friends in life," I said while staring out the window, looking at nothing in particular.

He glanced my way with a sorrowful look. I didn't need his pity. I needed real good people around me. That was a non-negotiable. Life is too difficult to be around people who make you feel less than, miserable, or inadequate.

Michael and I hadn't yet made our relationship official; we continued to date casually. The subject of his ex frequently surfaced. I suppose I wanted reassurance that he had genuinely moved on from her. By "moved on," I mean completely, irreversibly done. I'd rather not encounter her at all if she isn't willing to meet with me face-to-face. So, I presented an ultimatum. Familiar with the destructive power of jealousy, I aimed to sidestep any perilous games. My primary rule was simple: don't toy with my feelings. Establishing boundaries was essential; otherwise, people might take advantage of you, a lesson I was learning through my interactions with Gia. It was a peculiar dynamic; on one hand, I admired her relationship with Vince, yet on the other, I felt a twinge of envy toward Vince. Eventually, I realized that while she might be Vince's prize and Michael's "best friend," she was becoming an irritant in my life. I hoped she would step back, both promptly and respectfully.

***

The Next Evening…

It was our second official date, and I anticipated something thoughtful. Michael was incredibly generous and open-hearted when it came to romance. I eagerly awaited what he had planned for this outing. He genuinely seemed to enjoy our time together, and our chemistry was palpable. I found myself yearning for his company when he wasn't around. We were complete contrasts: he was talkative while I was more reserved; he stood tall, and I was petite. He had a lean build while I was fuller. His skin was darker, whereas mine had a caramel hue. Yet, we seemed to fit perfectly, complementing each other in just the right ways.

"Alright, babe, you ready?" he said, waiting patiently for me to get ready.

"Yeah, I'm ready," I said, putting the final touches on my make up. I wore a blue dress with Uggs, and my hair was styled in an Afro. I felt like a black queen.

"You look so good," he said from the doorway of my room in my mother's home.

"Thank you, babe!" I said, knowing that I did indeed.

"You get the room?" I asked.

"Yeah, I did. Gia said she could get us a discount this time, but I got it," he said, scratching his head.

Hmmm. "I'm sure she couldn't," I said suspiciously.

It might have been sabotage, but I held that comment to myself. I shrugged, grabbed my duffel bag off the floor, and headed to the front door with Michael. The dogs chomped at his ankles as he walked by. My shitzu Charming hated Michael. Charming was my baby, but he was jealous of the time I was spending with Michael.

Can't you see that I'm trying to find you a decent father, Charming? I winked at Charming on my way out of the door. He had a worried look on his face, which was weird. Charming was a very easy going, loving dog.

"He can't stand me, " said Michael.

"No, he can't," I said, looking at Michael apologetically.

We arrived at the restaurant in thirty minutes. It was Denny's. Okay, sure, whatever. I didn't really mind Denny's; they had good breakfast food. Was it a cheap date? Certainly, but I wasn't upset. I ordered an omelet and a pancake while he chose a chicken sandwich. As we ate, we engaged in casual conversation. However, when the bill arrived, he glanced at me, slowly reaching for his wallet with a hint of hesitation on his face, making me wonder if he was reluctant to pay.

Pussy Policy #20: Don't feel guilty if a man is paying for your meals, especially if he asked you out. He should pay for the first couple of dates; then, doing half is okay.

"It's ok. I got it," I said, pulling out my wallet.

He happily slid his wallet back into his pocket.

"What are you doing?" I asked, peering at him like he had grown a second head.

"I thought you were offering to pay the tab…"

"You thought wrong," I said, laughing.

"Split the check, " I told the waiter as she walked by. She grabbed my card as he scrambled to pull his wallet back out.

He had to have even been out of his mind to think I was about to pay for our dinners.

Chapter 10

THE THANKS WE GIVE

"The thanks that we give lives on in the blessings that we receive, but sometimes those blessings are actually designed to be the Trojan horse."

-Sovereign Jane Jenkins

Jackson, Mississippi
November 23, 2017

Thanksgiving break was fast approaching, and I was excited to be able to spend more time with Michael. We typically got a week out of school for Thanksgiving, and I had a feeling that I would spend the majority of the time with him. Our connection was growing stronger. I was thankful to Gia for introducing us. "Would you come to Thanksgiving dinner with me?" Michael asked out of the blue while I was studying at the library. I panicked. That means he was asking me to meet his entire family. My palms grew sweaty as I texted Gia.

"SOS! He wants me to meet his peeps!" I texted Gia.

"Relax," she said. "It's just Turkey," she laughed. It wasn't just Turkey, and we both knew that, but I went along with the notion for as long as I could.

"Sure," I texted Michael nervously. Thanksgiving was only a week away. I was spending the holidays with my family anyway, might as well go up the street a few miles and meet his family. That weekend, I met the key people in his family, and he met mine. You know it's real if you meet my mama. We were getting closer, and I became nervous. The more time we spent together, the more I craved his body. His mouth. His lips. His tongue, etc.

That Wednesday of Thanksgiving break, I finally met Michael's brother. He had poked his head in the door while Michael and I were reading something on his phone regarding the upcoming Marvel movies series. We were both fans of the Marvel Universe. That was another plus about being with him. He simply got it. Nathan's head came into view. It was almost like he was a child, being sneaky and nosey at the same time.

"Hey," he said finally. Michael and I both glanced upwards.

"Hey," I said calmly. "How are you doing?"

"Good." Nathan walked into the room to shake my hand.

I laughed at the situation. He had this goofy but happy look on his face. I guess everyone was excited about the new girl.

Was his ex that bad? Everyone seemed to breathe a sigh of relief at the fact that Michael had a new girlfriend.

"What are y'all up to?" Nathan asked.

"Just looking into the Marvel movies."

"Oh, she's a fan? She's cool with me," Nathan said.

I laughed as I gave him a fist bump. Nathan seemed cool and low-pressure. Nathan was also a nurse. That's probably why his energy didn't alarm me. We were both *chill Bills.*

"Y'all not going to hug?" I asked, confused, as Nathan walked out without even touching Michael.

"No, we don't have that kind of a relationship."

My eyebrows furrowed.

What! What kind of family is this?

He shrugged and went back to looking at the list of movies. I looked at the door again as I heard Nathan close the guest bedroom. I shrugged my shoulders and went back to doing the same.

But seriously, what kind of brothers didn't hug after not seeing each other for over three months? It was weird to me. I had a loving and touching relationship with my family. I wanted the same for my children. I was determined to get just that.

***

The Next Day…

Thanksgiving Day had finally come around, and I was as nervous as could be about having dinner with Michael's family. I was confident I'd make a great impression, but I was naturally shy around new people. His brother seemed cool, but how would the rest of his family react to me? There was only one way to find out.

"You should get an STD test," I said during one of the Thanksgiving break days. I said during one of the Thanksgiving break days. He shrugged his shoulders, agreeing with me as we dined out. It was our seventh date, and he was giving me a great time. With every kiss, touch, embrace, and token of love, I was unaware of how deeply I was getting entwined. The intensity grew with each passing day.

I was ready to lose my virginity because I was tired of waiting. Would the RIGHT man ever show up? After all, any man can change in the blink of an eye. I wanted to live freely for once. Being a virgin my entire life had become a core part of my identity. However, I've always believed in protection.

Pussy Policy #21: Require a STD test before having sex with a new partner.

People lie—it's human nature. There are individuals out there deliberately spreading incurable diseases out of spite, angered because someone hurt them.

I paid for my food, and he didn't seem to have a problem with it, but I did. In truth, a man who loves you will wine and dine you until you become his and even afterward. Dating and keeping things fresh is a marathon, not a sprint.

Pussy Policy # 22: Require that a man invest in you by paying for your time; don't be a cheap commodity.

He assumed I didn't want a relationship where the man paid for everything. However, the truth was, I sought a healthy relationship with an unselfish, thoughtful man. Gifts were my love language, after all, and I felt neglected. He was becoming lazier and more selfish with each passing day — another red flag to add to the growing pile. I blinked away the doubts as I reflected on my mother's relationships with my step-father and biological father. My biological father was a millionaire who used money to control her. I didn't want a relationship like that. So, I had mistakenly believed that asserting my independence early in the relationship would lead to lasting love. Instead, it led to lasting resentment, stinginess, and selfishness. My mother always said, "The way you begin a relationship sets the tone for its entirety. It all depends on how you start it off." I could hear her voice echoing in my head for the hundredth time that week.

So, I had to take a stand on who should cover expenses. If he wanted my time, he was going to pay for it.

"I'm not paying for it," he stated emphatically as we drove to the church event the day after Thanksgiving.

"We'll see," I thought to myself, or he won't be getting his dick sucked. We were en route to his mother's annual church event, a banquet celebrating their faith. I agreed to attend out of politeness and respect for his mother. I wasn't a Jew, and I had no desire to convert. Michael claimed he was Christian, but the more time I spent with him, the clearer it became that he was uncertain about his beliefs. He even went as far as to label Christmas as a "pagan" holiday, seemingly to curry favor with his mother. I raised an eyebrow at his audacity. He even suggested I buy his mother a gift. Why would I do that if she didn't even celebrate Christmas?

Pussy policy #23: Date someone with the same faith, so it won't be an arguing point later on.

He glanced over at me while driving and said, "I failed the test. I failed miserably. I've never felt like this before." Gia, Vince, Michael, and I were all seniors preparing to graduate from college. This failure would mean he'd have to stay in school for another semester, which heightened my anxiety. "I'm sorry. Does that mean you won't pass the class?" I asked, my voice tinged with nervousness, already formulating a breakup speech in my mind even though we weren't officially together.

"Not that test, babe. The STD test," he laughed. I didn't find it particularly amusing. He opened the glove compartment and handed me his test results as proof—all negative. I was secretly relieved since I had already put my mouth on that thing. It might not be the right thing to focus on, but I'm just being honest.

"Okay, good for you." I wanted to make sure he didn't misinterpret that as a green light for further intimacy. He was mistaken if he thought so. We both still had work to do in our relationship.

∗∗∗

We had another outing at Gia's. This time, he asked permission. Gia came to the door with a right-sided black eye. I looked at Michael, and Michael looked at me quietly, observing the apartment behind her. Nothing seemed out of the ordinary, and it didn't appear to have been a fight in the living room area. She seemed like she was in high spirits, but I wanted to ask what happened to her eye. I felt myself becoming agitated from my past traumas. I had watched my mom go through abuse. I didn't want to see her go through the same thing.

"How's it going," Michael asked, breaking the ice as we settled into a comfortable spot in her apartment. She wore a robe, and despite her black eye, she looked delicious. I grew up with brothers, so my masculinity kicked into high gear with pheromones. It was partially because I felt she was getting abused and partially because of attraction. This was totally messed up. But I couldn't help but ogle at the nipple print of her robe as she talked with her legs crossed upright in her chair. I crossed my legs, trying to quell that frustration.

"What happened to your face?" Michael blurted out, unable to help himself and thankfully breaking her spell on me. I swallowed hard, not wanting things to grow uncomfortably awkward. She looked taken aback, and I looked at the cabinets in the kitchen to not catch the truth of the matter. I didn't want to think ill of Vince, but I needed to know. So, I let Michael do the heavy lifting.

"My face?" She laughed, grabbing her right eye. "Oh, this? I did this this morning while opening up the cabinet too quickly. I bruise easily. I'm anemic after all," she said while laughing, implying that what we were thinking was far from the truth. I wasn't sure if I believed her, but one thing was certain: she needed more clothes on.

Her thigh peeked out as she crossed her legs at the table while Michael and I sat on the couch. 'Was she doing this on purpose, or am I going crazy and reading the situation all wrong?' I looked over to Michael, and he seemed oblivious to the charms that she was strumming with her actions. She didn't pay me any mind at all and continued to ramble about some frivolous things regarding computer engineering versus medical school. I couldn't care less. I 'accidentally' lasered in on her breasts. I could admit I was sexually attracted to women, but I would not consider marrying a woman. However, looking never hurt anyone, so my eyes spoke volumes while she rambled on.

"Right, Neka," Gia said while staring at me. I blinked, looking confused because I had no idea why the conversation suddenly turned towards me.

"Um, Yeah, sure!" I said in confusion. Gia laughed, knowing how airy and in my head I was. She knew I had heard nothing they said.

"I had lost my mind!" Gia exclaimed. "That relationship changed me forever. I was, like, crazy over him. I took care of him and everything!"

"Who is him?" I asked.

"Chris, my ex. Exactly a year after we broke up, he began blowing my phone up. I had to block him on every platform. He was asking if I had moved on, which I had! So, there was nothing that we had to discuss. He decided to sleep with his ex a day after sleeping with me, and he returned and broke up with me again. I cried for a few months. It was so bad. I was a mess. It was to the point that my granny said, 'Gee Gee! I can't take it anymore. Stop crying over that good for nothin little boy.'" You gotta love old Southern Grannies; they always tell it like it is.

"Janeka, you really should wait until marriage," Gia said. I blinked oddly, wondering how the conversation turned towards me. She was warning me from some unseen hurt. I wish I had heeded her warning.

"SHHH! SHHH!" Michael tried to hush her. He clearly wanted the benefits of intimacy before marriage. Of course he did, yet he didn't even want to pay for my hot dog. *Boy, bye,* I thought to myself. If I did decide to sleep with him, it would be on my terms. I didn't envision a future with him; he wasn't my type. I needed someone I could proudly be with every day. I shouldn't have given him a chance. While I did have feelings for him, I wasn't wholly invested. Not yet, anyway. Maybe in time. Perhaps, just perhaps.

"I'm serious, Neka. You're a queen, a prize. Make him wait for your essence—your most prized possession." As I listened to her, I felt conflicted. The pleasure from mere foreplay was so euphoric; I could only imagine what full intimacy with him would be like.

I smiled and nodded, acknowledging her concerns. It wasn't that I was ignoring her advice; it was that life was so unpredictable. I wanted to know what all the excitement was about. When would I be ready? I wasn't sure. One thing was certain: it wouldn't just be about Michael. It would be about my experience as a human, a primal being, and a woman. I craved that experience. I desired it more than I craved chocolate brownies, and I *adored* chocolate brownies.

"I hear you, girl. Where is Chris now?"

"Shit, I don't know. It beats me. He's probably with the same chick he left me for because I no longer want him," she said, laughing.

"Good for you!" I said. " That serves him right! That asshole!" I said. I was appalled that anyone would treat my girl like that. My friend-girl, that was.

Michael sat quietly, half listening, half bored of the conversation, but it was between me and her at that point. So I couldn't blame him. It wasn't his conversation or his warning. He had been hurt before himself after his ex-girlfriend broke up with him the second time. He had begged and pleaded the first time around, and she belittled him and called him less than a man. "That's weak. You're weak!" she told him. A little boy. She thought that would make him straighten up his act, so she used to break up with him, ghost him, and then dangle the relationship like a carrot as a cruel punishment. She didn't anticipate me coming into the picture the second time around that she broke up with him and that he would hit it off with me. Well, I was happy to rain on her parade.

Chapter 11

PUSSY IS A PRIVILEGE

"Dear Virgin, the world is oblivious of your strength but often learns of your importance not long after the traumas of life have touched them."
-**Sovereign Jane Jenkins**

Jackson, Mississippi
December 8, 2017

I sat on Michael's bed in his room, awaiting his return with the popcorn so we could start the movie. His family had an unusual affinity for films. I had never watched TV this frequently. When I was in elementary school, my father would often walk into the room, turn off the TV, and hand me a newspaper. He'd instruct me to read it until I understood the content and then summarize it for him once he returned from his wealth-generating activities. He was a strict man, and I didn't grasp his reasoning back then. He viewed TV as a time-waster, something that could be addictive and manipulative. He didn't want me to be influenced by it; he aimed to teach me to think for myself, albeit within certain boundaries. Nowadays, I usually prefer settling down with a good book. The challenge was that Michael didn't share this love for reading. To compromise, I found myself watching movies with him more often than I'd like.

I digress. I used to be too engrossed in living my life to watch TV so frequently, but by that time, I had significantly adjusted my pace for Michael. I began to understand the stark contrast between our energies: I was inherently high-energy, while he exuded a slower, more relaxed vibe. Standing in Michael's room, I was momentarily puzzled by what he was saying.

"Rene reached out to me to say she did want me back," Michael said while sitting on his bed.

"Why are you even still talking to her? Better yet, why are we still talking about her?" I said, bewildered.

"Rene and I are still friends," he said emphatically.

"Where are the messages?" I said, looking around for his phone.

"I deleted them," he said. I could feel my eyebrow quirk and my distrust rise. This was becoming fishy-er by the second.

"Why did you do that?"

"Because I felt guilty for replying, and I talked to Gia about it. She made me feel like I had done something wrong," he said.

I put my hand on my head to avoid reaching his way because I was becoming dangerously frustrated.

"What do you mean y'all are still 'friends'?" I said, annoyed, and my voice rose a few octaves.

"We have a dog together. The dog used to be hers, but he escaped a few times, and I had to go catch him. She couldn't control him, so now I have him."

"Excuse me for not giving a damn. If she can't sit down with me and have a civil conversation, then that friendship has to cease, or we're done."

"But we've been together for five years. It's not that simple."

"So, go be with her then," I said, ready to get up and walk out the door.

"Wait, ok," he said.

"Ok. What?"

"Ok, I'll ask her to have lunch with you again, and if she says, 'no,' I'll eventually let it go."

"No, you WILL let it go because she already said no. "

"I don't have those feelings for her anymore."

"Letting it go should be easy because you moved on, right?" I said, pointing to myself.

"Right," he said in defeat.

"Good."

"I'll give you my password to my phone. So, you know no games or dishonest actions are going on. I have nothing to hide. No funny business," he said, handing me his phone. I shrugged my shoulders, took it, and went through it without shame or guilt. I'm grown. I'm unapologetically me and doing things my way. I waited 22 years to get here. He offered, and I accepted.

"Just give it a chance," he said.

"Would it be ok if I gave a random guy a chance? Since we're giving out ridiculous chances freely," I said.

"That's different."

"No, it's not. It's a man who's not related to me trying to get close. That's a red flag for a relationship. And you claim that's what you've been wanting. If I have to drop my guard, you have to get rid of your ex. Period." He fell silent, knowing he was losing this battle. I shouldn't have had to state the obvious, but there I was, doing it anyway. I made it clear that this behavior would not be tolerated. He promised me that he'd let her go. But would he? Only time will tell. I remained agitated for the rest of the night after that argument. Silently, I took him to Miss E, who had a workout session that evening. I knew she would push us hard, but I needed to vent my frustration and blow off steam. If this was what a relationship truly entailed, I wasn't sure I could handle it long-term. It was just exhausting. It felt like I was conversing with a child, not a grown man. I was on the verge of pressing the red button again; this was getting old.

Pussy Policy #24: Never give more than three chances for the same offense.

IT WAS ANOTHER MAJOR ARGUMENT, and I was far from happy. Miss E knew her stuff and made me feel so much stronger after every session. I also wanted to test out Michael's fitness. Could he grow with me? Could he keep up with me? Could he go with me physically, spiritually, emotionally, and metaphorically? Could he grow as a man? He seemed childlike most of the time, but I supposed most men gave off this same frustration. The workout only helped quell my frustrations slightly. I was still on edge and needed a good release. Once we returned from the gym, I allowed him to eat me out. He dove head-first into my pussy and ate it well. It was a mercy meal. I tried my best to maintain control, but it was useless as he held my thighs apart and tickled a particular spot with his tongue. I screamed for mercy. There was none.

Even after I orgasmed, he wouldn't stop. I guess that was the 'silent' but not so subtle 'I'm sorry.' I laughed at the simplicity of life. A simple orgasm solved lots of problems, even if only temporarily. Bill Clinton taught me that. He looked confused as to why I was laughing and upped the ante. He focused on one particular place that he knew drove me crazy while playing with my right nipple, which was extra sensitive. I had to make sure I didn't scream too loud because his parents were sleeping in the next room. Oh yeah, he still lived with his parents.

Typical college student shit, but there I was, hanging on for dear life at the tip of another orgasmic cliff, and he catapulted me over, and I felt everything at that moment. I even saw stars. However, I was still slightly on edge and wanted it all that night. I pulled out his erection, which was a good six and a half inches—the perfect size for me. I was tiny, and this was going to be an ordeal. I laid on my back as he tried four times to thrust through my hymen. She wasn't going easily. In fact, she was downright stubborn. I swallowed as the pain was hitting me all at once. It was like a sharp, invasive ache that needed a robe scratched, but he wasn't quite getting through. I was so wet that it wasn't the lack of juices; the intensity of my legs resisting and the grip of my vaginal muscles showed him no mercy. I guess he was hurting himself because he had to guide himself, so he would bend it while trying to get through.

"Relax," he said, pushing forward and trying his luck again. This time, after his persistent pushing, he broke through, and it was like a damn broke apart. I felt so full. I didn't know what else to do, so I just held on for the ride. His thrusts became ragged and rushed. I had to protect my head from coming in contact with the wall, so I anchored myself against it while also trying to prevent his bed from making a grating sound on the wall, alerting his parents of our newest activities.

Pussy Policy #25: Never reward a man after he disrespects you.

"Damn, you're so tight," he muttered.

"Thank you," I said with a curt smile to keep from screaming out loud and waking his parents. He was sweating all over me and showed no signs of stopping. Five minutes passed, and he couldn't hold it anymore. He pulled out and released himself into the condom.

"I'm a woman now," I said with a smile on my face while lying on my back, staring up at the ceiling. Only the TV illuminated the room, so I couldn't see the look on Michael's face.

"Oh god," he said, laughing at my humor. I was serious, though. I was a woman now. The hymen was destroyed. I could move to the next chapter of my life: 'sex on the regular.' I slept overnight against his parents' wishes, but my car was not outside of the house, so they were under the impression that I had already gone home. I hadn't. In fact, we fucked all night and day over the remainder of Thanksgiving break once they left for work, just in case that sneaky hymen of mine decided to come back with a vengeance. I was game for more and received a lot more almost constantly that week. I was addicted to the high. That feeling was unmatched. That hit of dopamine was nothing like I had ever felt. That was a super vine twisting up into my soul with thorns, polluting me by changing my brain's chemical makeup. It was now a full-blown soul tie, and I continued to let him sink deeper into my soul. He seemed honorable; however, at that point, anyone with a clean erection would do.

"Are you satisfied?" he asked.

"Yes. I am," I said, lying there happily. I finally had a healthy sex life. Sex was important, but Mama said men often used sex to charm women, while women used love and physical attraction to charm men. It was the dopamine hit. The rush of the drug was overriding my system to the point that I forgot that he was still intent on holding on to his ex-girlfriend. Lust will make you do some crazy things, I tell you. That's why I say live your life but learn the lessons.

"Just so we're clear, we're still friends with benefits…"

"Understood," he said with a triumphant edge to his voice.

I fell into a deep, coma-like sleep for the first time in my life. I wasn't usually a heavy sleeper, so it was surprising. I even remembered my dream. It wasn't necessarily a pleasant one and was about Gia for some reason. It had a sexual nature, which left me perplexed. Those were the thoughts lurking deep within my subconscious mind. I couldn't stop the thoughts and images, but I could suppress the feelings, especially around her. Perhaps all those pheromones ignited an inferno of lust within me. It began to dominate my system. My desire for sex grew to the point where I considered paying for a hotel room myself. Michael didn't have a steady job, but I had some savings from my student tutoring. I made certain sacrifices in the name of 'lust.'

"I love you," he said.

"I love you, too," I began to respond every time we parted ways from then on.

Pussy Policy #26: Never love a man more than you love yourself.

Was it real love? It might've been for a time, especially while our intimacy was strong. His sex was magnetic, and I was ready to indulge every time, which was becoming a problem.

***

The next day…

Michael and I met Gia at Applebee's for dinner this particular night. It was becoming our favorite hang-out spot. I was still reeling from the night before, but I wouldn't mention it just yet to Gia. It was still my personal life, and I was still analyzing how I felt about opening up that part of myself. It was one of the most memorable experiences of my life, and I wanted to cherish it for as long as I could, even if I did regret it later.

I was more afraid of Gia being right. What if I should have waited? What if I had just made the biggest mistake of my life? There were so many 'what if's' that my mind was overloaded. I decided to just stay in the moment. My heart was racing, and I'm sure I was trying to make room for the fact that I was no longer a virgin. My twenty-two-year identity was no more. I was a grown woman.

"How did your weeks go?" Gia asked directly.

"Fine!" I said with a little more enthusiasm than necessary.

Gia looked at me with a strange expression. I wondered if Michael had blabbed.

"Mine was good. I had a lot of homework to do, and I worked with my dad in some gardens. Landscaping is an art, but I feel like our clients don't respect us. Half of them don't even know our names," Micheal said with a thoughtful look.

I could tell something was heavy on his mind, but I didn't realize it was that. I wondered why he didn't tell me that in private. It seemed like a heart-to-heart, one-on-one conversation was needed for this topic.

"You feel like you're not respected as a gardener?" Gia asked.

"I feel like I'm not respected as a black man," Michael said.

Gia and I glanced at each other briefly. We sympathized with him, but we couldn't relate to him.

"They looked right at us and didn't speak to us. They acted like we were invisible. I'm sick of it," Michael said, frustrated.

Michael and his father had darker skin and shared similar facial features. However, Michael stood taller than his father, and, in my opinion, his father's features suited his face better. His father was a jolly man, always loud, boisterous, and direct. He seemed to be perpetually laughing and enjoying himself. I genuinely adored his father. On the other hand, his mother struck me as a bit peculiar. She was reserved and deeply committed to her Judaistic temple. She rarely left the house and was consistently at church on Saturdays. While it wasn't my place to comment—perhaps that was how she coped with the loss of her mother—I found myself making judgments. After all, people are people.

"Do you think he would have spoken had you been white?" I asked.

"I'm sure of it. I get it all the time. It's like we're viewed as subhuman because of the color of our skin," he said.

Gia and I were two lighter-skinned women in Jackson, Mississippi. Gia and I looked at each other again, not confused, but definitely mentally challenged with the subject. We didn't get it. Gia was more fair-skinned than I, so she damn sure didn't get it. I understood the racial side of the puzzle because my stepdad was white, and my mother was black. I saw the looks everywhere we went. It was concerning at first because I was not used to it. After a while, I didn't notice the looks anymore, either due to being extremely nearsighted or just not giving a damn anymore. Either way, I understood that race was still a factor. My parents were my world and my supreme council. I didn't care about the rest of the world. I only cared about my family at the moment.

"Michael, you don't have long as a gardener. One more semester of school, and we're there," Gia said, placating him. I could tell it wasn't helping him. He needed reassurance for his mental health. I knew he needed something else.

"Michael, you're a wonderful worker, and because you're a wonderful person, you're going to find your place and your tribe soon enough that's going to accept you for you. It takes time. It's not going to be something that happens right off the bat. Just like it took you time to find me," I said, winking at Gia. Gia smirked at the comment because she was the reason that we were there.

Michael looked at me and smiled. Judging by his reaction, I must have said something that resonated with him. He seemed comforted.

"You mean it took me *this* long to introduce y'all," she corrected, laughing.

"That's what I said," I replied with a sheepish smile, glancing at Gia.

We all laughed, reminiscing about the events that had led up to that day. It seemed our meeting was destiny.

"I'm glad you introduced us," I told Gia. Overhearing the comment, Michael smiled. It was evident that his ego and pride were swelling with happiness at that moment.

Gia leaned back in her chair, observing us interact silently for a moment. She appeared pleased and content with the fact that we were together, at least for the time being. It felt right that we had reached this point, comfortable in each other's company. That was a promising sign. I truly loved Michael by then. Sure, there were moments when he tested my patience to the limit, but my love for him never waned. I hoped he felt the same about me and prayed that he did. I didn't want to experience heartbreak. As our food arrived at the table, the conversation flowed.

"I'm glad he finally told you about Rene contacting him. I told him he should. If he hadn't, and you found out some other way, it could have jeopardized your relationship," Gia commented as she took a bite of her salad.

Silence ensued over the table as I looked over at Michael. I instantly became pissed off because:

- That should have been a no-brainer.
- Gia should not have known about that.
- That was inappropriate for her to bring up at that table.
- That was friendship talk.
- He deleted the messages.

I put down my fork for a minute because I had lost my appetite. I looked over at him, and he could tell I was absolutely pissed all over again. He had the 'uh oh' look on his face once again.

Chapter 12

THE GIFT OF GIVING

"Giving is the tried and true mark of freedom."
-**Sovereign Jane Jenkins**

Kosciusko, Mississippi
December 25, 2018

Before we knew it, Christmas arrived, and I found myself at the house of my eldest brother, Darren. Michael was on his way to visit and meet more of my family. He seemed committed enough to drive hours away from home just to see me in a foreign county. This county was the back-door, country-woods type with no cell phone service. I had to give him credit; the guy was brave. Unfortunately, I was terribly sick that day. I battled a fever, chills, nausea, vomiting, and a persistent cough. Despite feeling miserable, I remained at my brother's house. On Christmas Eve, my two brothers and I had indulged in watching classics like "*The Christmas Story*" and "*Home Alone*." My middle older brother, Chayne, slept on a blow-up mattress beside me with his girlfriend, Christie. Darren, sixteen years my senior, was more like a second father to me than a brother. We had a tradition of spending every Christmas together. Being in each other's company always brightened our spirits. However, that particular morning found me in bed, shivering uncontrollably.

A knock came at the door, and Darren answered the door.

"Hey! How are you doing?" I heard my brother say.

"Hey, I'm Michael," I heard Michael say.

Darren opened the door wider to let him in while I was still lying in bed.

"Hey!" I said, peeking out from under the cover.

"Hey," he said, looking sheepish because I was still in bed in my PJs.

I had no reason to be ashamed, even though I was terribly sick. Michael quietly took a seat at the back of the room, waiting patiently for the food to be ready. Eventually, I mustered the strength to get out of bed and freshen up before our meal. My stomach was in such turmoil that I wreaked havoc in the bathroom. To my chagrin, there was no air freshener available. To make matters worse, right after I stepped out, Chayne entered the bathroom.

"Who-Wee! What did you eat?" my middle brother practically yelled out loud; I was beyond embarrassed.

Michael laughed too loud for my liking, and I sent him a death stare in exchange.

'Bastards!' I thought to myself.

"Man, shut up. I'm not feeling the best," I said to Chayne. Of course, he never made the situation better, always worse.

I walked over to fix my plate after making sure that my face was clear of any evidence of my earlier activity of blowing my nose.

"What are you doing?" Darren asked, looking at me directly.

"Fixing my plate," I said in confusion.

"Fix his plate first," he said while nodding towards Michael. I glanced at Michael, and he paused on the edge of his seat in his attempt to get up.

"Huh!" I said, bewildered. I was beyond confused because why would I fix his plate? His feet aren't broken. I wasn't raised in a two-parent household, and at my momma's house, we always ate first, and the man served himself. I guess that's the result of trauma.

Nonetheless, I was baffled. However, I didn't argue. My older brother seemed to want the respect due to a father while retaining the title of 'brother.' It didn't add up, but to avoid an argument, I humored him. "Fix his plate first because he's a man and your guest," Darren said sternly. I suddenly felt like a child again and couldn't help but frown in response. I gave Darren a baffled look. I was the one who was sick; he should have been attending to me. However, since I wasn't the one who prepared the meal and Darren was the cook, I bit my tongue and abided by his rules.

Pussy Policy #27: If he has not made you his wife, don't treat him like a husband, not yet anyway.

I methodically prepared Michael's meal, navigating the serving area. Walking over to where Michael sat on the couch, I set his plate down gently on the table before him. I shot him a stern look that clearly conveyed, "Don't get used to this." He caught the message loud and clear. Then, I returned to assemble my own meal while the cheerful chatter among my family continued. I was irked, as my brother Darren was quite traditional. His wife always served him his meals. I didn't believe it was my responsibility to serve a boyfriend; in my opinion, only a husband merited such an act. Regardless, I kept these thoughts to myself and sat beside Michael, eating in silence.

That Christmas, I went the extra mile for Michael. I bought him brand-new shoes — gray and red Nikes, with red being his favorite color. I also gifted him gray work boots. In return, he presented me with a blue Calvin Klein bag. I was elated, nearly moved to tears. It was exquisite and absolutely suited for me. I believed that he would reciprocate with similar energy if I extended kindness towards him. I felt he had truly listened to me this time. Even though I had showered him with numerous gifts by then, I was content with just the bag. While I valued words of affirmation, physical touch, and acts of service, gifts held a special place in my heart. In simpler terms: "Show Me the Money!" He didn't earn much as a lawn servicer and gardener. Still, I'd be damned if I was going to provide my time, intimacy, and affection without him reciprocating through meal expenses and gestures of kindness. He usually covered our meals without grumbling. However, he occasionally hesitated when it came to gifting, leading me to occasionally pull back on intimacy. He did make more of an effort over time, though it sometimes felt insufficient to me. My family seemed to have taken a liking to him. After unwrapping our presents, we were all in high spirits. We captured moments with an old Polaroid camera. Michael and I genuinely reveled in each other's company, with the room filled with laughter and warmth. Michael's family didn't celebrate Christmas, given his mother's Judaism beliefs that labeled it a "pagan" holiday. That was perfectly alright by me. In the long run, it meant fewer holiday gifts to purchase. I shrugged it off.

Pussy Policy #28: Never go above and beyond for a man that would not do the same for you.

***

Two weeks later…

I sat on the bed, staring into a blank space as Michael sat beside me. He had cum inside me accidentally. I was mortified because I knew better but failed to do better.

"We should have used a condom…" I blamed myself and Michael; however, it was me. It was completely my fault because it was my body. This could derail all my plans, my goals, and my aspirations. I hadn't even finished school yet, but I was on the brink of motherhood. My mother was going to be so disappointed in me.

"But I can't feel anything with a condom…" he said.

My head snapped up, and I stared at him in anger.

"Wow," I said, "I don't have a ring on my finger, but you want to 'raw dog' me and get pregnant…" I said, staring at him.

"It was an accident. You crossed your legs, and you're so tight," he said as if that explained everything.

"Never mind that! What if I'm pregnant!?!" I screamed.

He sat that and stared at me back until a lightbulb went off. "Plan B!"

Great idea!

We both jumped up at the same time and scrambled to get our clothes on to head to the late-night drug store. Luckily, they had one left. We agreed to go half on the pill since we were both equally responsible for the slip-up. I didn't want to be on birth control because I didn't want the hormones causing havoc on my body, but something had to give. Condoms need to be added to this equation. I gulped down the pill with the water bottle in the car, praying that the seed would not take root.

Why was I even having sex with him? I deserved a ring. Everyone told me to wait, but I was hardheaded. Now, I'm up at three in the morning, popping the morning-after pill. What a life!!

Chapter 13

RELATIONSHIP-PHOBIC

"The act of commitment buffers the pain of loss, which often becomes the reality of hesitancy."
~**Sovereign Jane Jenkins**

Hattiesburg, Mississippi
January 10, 2018

While walking into my dorm room juggling grocery bags, I was on the phone with Michael. It seems that when you're deep into a situationship, the world suddenly views you as a novelty, and numerous individuals attempt to pursue you. At least, that was my experience. I grappled with my multitude of bags when a handsome man strolled past.

"Hey, beautiful," he greeted. "Need some help with those?"

I was still on the phone with Michael. We weren't "official," so why did I feel guilty craving this stranger's attention? Perhaps it was the allure of something new; everyone is drawn to shiny, new distractions.

"Yes, I'll take the help," I replied without a second thought. I enjoyed playing the damsel in distress and reveled in the attention. Why would I refuse when I genuinely needed assistance?

Michael's side of the call went silent. I sensed he was hanging onto every word.

"I'm Chad," the stranger introduced himself. "Honestly, I'm a student here. I major in math. What about you?"

"Hi Chad! I'm Janeka, and I'm a nursing major." In our program, no one would dare claim to be a nurse outright. Doing so was akin to tempting fate, given the program's rigor. It was reputed to be the most challenging in Mississippi, and there I was, either honored or ill-fated, to be a part of it.

Chad was an interesting character. He was attractive with almond-shaped sultry eyes, curly hair, and the perfect goatee decorating his face. I was instantly turned on and couldn't resist his conversation.

"That's cool," he said, grabbing the case of water from my trunk as we headed into the building. I could hear Michael breathing in the background over the phone. I could also hear Gia and Vince chattering in the background. He was over at their house. For what? Just hanging out. He was always 'just hanging out.' No sense of direction, urgency, or calling was present in his life. Red flag number eight. Chad seemed chatty and chipper as we walked to my room. I opened the door, not welcoming him in, but he had a case of water, so he stepped over the threshold behind me to put down the water.

"Nice place," he said, looking around my sparse yet simple dorm room. For me, simplicity was best, and that's how I lived my life. It was a wonderful philosophy that I had developed over the years. I had books all over the place, which would become my norm well into adulthood. Chad seemed genuinely interested, but I had some studying to do, and I'm sure he did as well.

"Can I give you my number?"

"Sure," I said, pulling out my phone, trying not to hang up on Michael, but I eventually had to in order to get Chad's number. I tried putting Michael on mute and switching over, but that only resulted in him hearing pressing buttons. So, I hung up deadpan. Again, we weren't an item, and Chad might have been the one. Only time would tell, but all's fair in love and war.

"I texted you."

"Good, I'll be in touch, " I said, winking.

"The pleasure was all mine, ma'am."

Chad left the room, and the door to my room slowly closed. I could feel my hormones raging again in reaction to his physique. He was short but muscular. He had a solid body, and his muscles were my Achilles heel.

Then, thoughts of Michael surfaced. A wave of guilt washed over me when I considered that Gia and Vince might have overheard the entire episode. In the larger picture, it shouldn't matter, yet I found myself inexplicably craving their validation. Perhaps because they self-proclaimed themselves the "It Couple." However, in my opinion, one can't be an 'It Couple' unless others see it that way too. Such is the psychology of it all. They often played the role of sage advisors regarding other people's relationships. Their influence was palpable. Even I, not in a relationship, felt its weight. Imagine that!

My phone vibrated with a message from Michael.

"What happened?"

"Chad helped me bring in my groceries."

"You got his number."

"Yes, he seemed friendly enough."

"Why would you do that?"

"Why not?" I said, it was tempting to point out the nature of our relationship.

He then called me.

"Uh, Oh. Time for damage control," I said aloud at no particular body.

"Is he still there?"

"No. He dropped my groceries and left soon after."

"But you got his number.."

"That wasn't a crime last time I checked."

"Do you know how that makes me look? Gia and Vince heard the whole ordeal." I was frustrated and irrevocably annoyed now because, unlike Gia and Vince, we weren't committed to each other. I wasn't one to be tied down. I was a self-proclaimed single woman taking life by storm, which is what I preferred. I understood that once you were locked down, you were mentally, physically, and spiritually off the market. I intended to stay on the market for as long as possible. I was only twenty-two, after all.

"You're taking me for granted. Don't."

"What are you talking about? We are just friends. I can't get other people's numbers?"

"No. Because you know I want more than that. What you did tonight hurt me." I felt a sinking feeling of guilt in the pit of my stomach. Then came the pain of regret. I had to be the empath and see things from his side of view. It appeared as if I was playing him because he was paying for dates and spending money on gas to drive one and a half hours away to visit me. I felt more guilty as the seconds ticked by, and sadness overcame me because I was conflicted. I told him I didn't want a relationship, but he insisted on breaking down the gilded wall of my heart. I was naturally a giver and never wanted to cause him pain.

"I'm sorry," I said, resolving that I was fucking that all the way up. "It won't happen again."

"Why did you do it? Do you want him? Were you attracted to him?"

"No, I'm just used to the attention and getting people's numbers…" I said, feeling horrible. Tears of drama were streaming down my face as a sympathy ploy. Oh, yes. I was not above crying. I didn't like that feeling and was genuinely sorry, but I was ready to give up on this.

"Ok," he said, reading that I was genuinely sorry. It was my first situationship/relationship if that's what the kids were calling it nowadays. He videochatted me once he returned home to his house, causing me to voice my true feelings at that moment.

"I'm not ready for a relationship. Graduation is coming up, and this is too much. Nursing school is stressful enough. Let's just put a hold on this and possibly pick it up later. I'm sorry again for what I did. I just need to focus on my studies. Finals are coming up, along with the Christmas break. Let's just focus on graduating for now."

Looking back, I knew I wanted to keep my options open with Chad, so I didn't worry about Michael's feelings, but I felt somewhat guilty because I had embarrassed him in front of Gia and Vince.

"Stop apologizing," he said. It was over. He was ready to change the subject, but my eyes were still red from my crying spell. Although I was sympathetic to his cause, I still wanted to explore things with Chad, so I kept Chad's number. Of course, I was not going to tell Michael that. 'What he did not know…' "Y'all know how the saying goes…."

I texted Gia then, not wanting her to think I was a harlot. "What are your thoughts on the situation?"

"I think you should make it clear what your intentions are with Michael. He's a good man and does not deserve to be hurt. You need to get it together."

"I know. I know," I said thoughtfully. The truth was I was not used to being on the hot seat; it felt like I had to bare my soul and confess my sins to get out of it.

"Just take it slow, but give it a real chance. At this point, y'all are still not official, but to keep him around, he will need more as a man sooner or later."

She was right, and I hated it. I swallowed, not liking anything, a swirling inferno of confusion in my head and my heart. Wait! My heart? When did it step into this mess? "Oh, shit," I thought to myself after Gia's pep talk.

My phone vibrated a short time later.

"It was nice meeting you." Oh, Chad. You'll get me in a world of trouble and don't even know it. It wasn't my place to tell you either. I'll keep him around for now. I might need help with groceries again or a jump for my car. Michael lived more than an hour away. 'What's the worst that could happen?' I needed to make my intentions clear, but I also needed to see how I felt about Chad.

The next day, I was minding my business, studying in the library, and still reeling from the night before. It was my first breakup, and I was ready to call it quits. It was too much to be committed to just one person. My options were remaining open.

My phone vibrated as I was flipping through my nursing notes.

"Hey, I'm outside your dorm with note cards. Let's study!" the message read.

"What!" I said out loud in the library. I looked around to try to see if I disturbed anyone. It was only me, thank God. I was taken aback and disgruntled. He wasn't hearing me.

"No, you are not!" I said in disbelief. "Why did you drive all this way? That's time and gas wasted."

"It's not a waste. Come outside, please."

"I'm at the library."

"Where's the library?"

"Don't worry about it," I said, packing up my things. "I'm coming."

I made my way back up to my dorm from the library, about a fifteen-minute walk from the library. Once Micheal's car came into view, he stepped outside, holding up some note cards.

"Let's study!" he said before I could reach him. I gawked in disbelief. Was he serious? Where did this man come from? I was silent as I led the way back to my dorm, still clearly in shock. He had brought pens, notecards, and highlighters to help us study. I threw the note cards on top of my desk and kissed him deeply.

"Babe, I didn't come here for this," he said. But I wanted it, and what Mama wanted, Mama got. I pulled out his stiff erection, and I did not have to do much of anything. I just went for it and sucked the life out of him. I gave head like I never did before to show him my appreciation. Once he finally had enough, he turned me around and pushed down my pants and underwear.

"Condom," I said as he was entering me raw.

"BABE, it's fine. I'm clean, and I love you," he said while thrusting into me without an ounce of protection. I could feel the ties tightening again around my soul, strengthening like the roots of a pucker wood tree. I swallowed as I held on to the desk for dear life. He was 6'4", but somehow, he contorted his body to match my height from behind. He beat it up and beat it up well. The passion took me aback. It had been a while for him, and I was convenient. He finished, and I silently cursed myself because I was giving him everything on a silver platter, and he still had not truly proven himself. I was making foolish decisions. I needed a wake-up call.

I tried not to scream out too loud because I still lived in a dorm room after all. I had no desire to face campus security within the next few minutes.

He must've done something right, because I then changed my password to his so we'd have the same iphone password. That was true trust and open communication. I wanted to start out on a good note with this relationship, so I rolled the dice and trusted. Secrets kill relationships and people. I didn't want to be another statistic, so I guessed I'd have to kill my relationship with Chad. It was still new to me, but I really wanted this thing with Michael to work. I knew the sacrifice had to be made.

Before he left, he wrote 'Misses Downs' on the back of one of my note cards and left it underneath my nursing book. My face turned beet red. That was his last name. I was falling deeper, and I knew it.

Pussy Policy #29: **A man's actions should always match up with his words.**

A week before Valentine's Day, I was excited because I had never had a good Valentine's Day. I finally would have gifts, love, affection, acts of service, physical touch, words of affirmation, and quality time to satisfy all of my requirements/expectations. But he quickly threw a bucket of ice-cold water on my dreams. "What do you mean you don't celebrate Valentine's Day?" I said, confused. Surely, he was joking, and I wasn't laughing. It was far from funny to me.

"I don't believe in it. What's the point of it? You spend money on useless stuff for what? It's a waste of money."

"Thoughtfulness and gifts are my love language," I said without remorse.

"You just want every day to be like Christmas," he said as if something was wrong with that.

My eyes began to sting, and he still didn't understand. I had given him my all, yet he remained self-centered, even when I shared myself with him without reservation. How was that just? He was treated to Christmas every day because I was his gift. But if I were to withdraw, would he object? An intriguing thought.

"Alright then. I don't believe in premarital sex. In fact, let's end this," I declared, hanging up the phone, both annoyed and exasperated.

In that moment, I recognized there was nothing more to discuss. The longer I stayed in this relationship, the unhappier I became.

Pussy Policy #30: Never be with a man that does not want to invest ENERGY, TIME, EFFORT, and MONEY into you; people don't value something when it's free.

There are some things that you simply should not have to ask for. Of course, he called back right then, but I honestly had no interest in continuing the conversation. He was never going to change.

Pussy Policy #31: A man treats you according to how he feels about you.

Don't put up with a broke man with no real intentions of truly loving you. Learn from the lessons and mistakes of others by walking away quickly. If he wanted to love you correctly, he would have. I sighed while sitting at my desk in my dorm after hanging up the phone. My feelings were genuinely hurt, so I did what I usually always did: I called my mama. She picked up on the first ring. Thank goodness.

"He said he didn't believe in Valentine's Day and didn't want to celebrate it."

"That's ridiculous. If he didn't want to spend any money, he should've just said that and left you alone."

"I know. That is the least he could have done," I said, annoyed while tears were in my eyes. I was a crybaby, yes, but that's how I felt at the time. If you don't want a relationship, then don't waste my time.

"Do you want to break up with him?"

"Honestly, we should since he's being so selfish. I deserve better than this."

"Well, what will you do about it?" my mother asked calmly. "How you begin a relationship is how it will be throughout it, but it gets worse from there. They start out high, then go lower in every aspect. So, if he's cheap now…Don't expect a decent wedding ring later."

"Oh, no!" I said aloud. That simply won't do.

"It's just the way it is, baby girl…."

"I don't know, mama. Why is dating this hard?"

"Janeka, that's the question of today. With all these problems so soon, are you sure you want to continue with this relationship? It's not like he's drop-dead gorgeous," she said.

"Momma, you know it's not about looks to me. On a scale of one to ten, how does he look to you?"

"I'll give him a six out of ten on a good day," my mother said.

I didn't find it amusing. This was my man we were talking about at this point.

"What if your children come out dark with his features?" she said.

"Mama! Stop it! I want my children to be healthy overall. Looks are not that important in the grand scheme of things. Character is."

"Well, judging by this conversation, his character is cheap," she said in a matter-of-fact voice.

I was angry then. Not at her, because she was right on that front, but at him. Maybe he'd change once he saw that I would truly ride for him. Maybe he'd get the message if I treated him how I would want to be treated. This thinking led me to another policy.

Pussy Policy #32: Never do more for a man than he does for you.

My phone vibrated right then as a message came through.

Messages:

Him: Hey, I'm sorry, but I just don't celebrate Valentine's Day.
Me: Ok, then we have nothing left to discuss.
Him: Why is it so important to you?
Me: Because I should not have to ask you for the bare minimum.
Him: That's the bare minimum?
Me: Yes, and you're setting the bar even lower.

I recognized that my words were harsh, but by then, my patience had worn thin, and I was tired of constantly defending him. That night, I had reached my limit with him. I placed my phone on the charger, set it to silent, and prepared for the upcoming day. I hoped that letting those words linger might make him reflect. Perhaps he would finally understand and give me space. As I evaluated our time together, his true nature became more evident. He behaved like a child, despite being twenty-four. He was frugal, inattentive, and at times, lacked excitement and motivation. Most troubling of all, he was holding me back. I had gained ten pounds since we started dating, and it had only been about four months. That was yet another warning sign for me, another strike against him.

Pussy Policy #33: Don't date a man that doesn't have a personal sense of self-direction or ambition. It'll feel like you're carrying him after a while.

All he wanted to do was sit around, watch TV, eat, sleep, and have sex. I was falling into these habits, too. It was comfortable, addictive, and routine. That wasn't truly who I was. I didn't want that at that stage of my life. I had just turned twenty-two. I needed something else. I needed action. I needed adventure. I needed excitement! That was not it.

Pussy Policy #34: Always have a life of your own outside of your relationship.

Why hadn't I left him by then? Why was I dedicating so much of my time to him? Why was I investing so deeply in him instead of prioritizing my own friends and my career? I couldn't quite understand it. In truth, I was still hung up on Gia and wanted to remain connected. Oh, the things we do for what we call 'love.' I was at a perplexing juncture in my life, a point that called for introspection. Who was I, really? What was the end goal? Did I genuinely want to be with him? I glanced at him, engrossed in his video game.

Fuck it!

"Pass me the other controller!" I exclaimed, sidestepping my inner turmoil. He looked up, startled, then handed me the controller, ensuring it was working right.

You show interest in your partner's interests, right? I decided to give it an honest try with him.

Chapter 14

VALENTINE'S DAY

"If the sex is good enough for you to remain with a cheating man, then you must pray for discernment and detachment firsthand."
~Sovereign Jane Jenkins

February 9, 2018

The day had finally arrived, and I was brimming with anticipation. Somehow, over the past few days, he'd managed to work his way back into my good graces. I had agreed to let him make amends, though I wasn't entirely sure why. He didn't deserve it, yet there I was, gearing up for our "big" date. I'd let my hair down, allowing it to blossom into an Afro. Dressed all in black with thigh-high boots, I felt confident.

Presentation counts. I'm not suggesting Michael was unattractive, but he certainly needed to invest in his wardrobe, hair maintenance, and hygiene. His habit of skipping brushing his teeth at night resulted in a less-than-fresh breath that I occasionally found overpowering. Still, I harbored genuine feelings for him. They had to be genuine, right? I must've felt something profound to have stayed with him that long. It had to be love... or was it? Maybe it was the thrill of finally being able to call someone "mine"? There was a certain satisfaction in saying, "He's my man." I've never been the lonely type, always able to find joy on my own. My quest was for self-fulfillment, not validation from someone else. I was seeking purpose and, along the way, got sidetracked by this diversion. But I digress...

I took one last look in the mirror before heading out. My hair framed my face perfectly, my makeup was impeccable, and my ensemble, complete with thigh-high boots, looked sharp. I felt primed for an evening out. Retrieving my duffel bag from the closet, I packed the essentials for our overnight stay. Michael had booked a hotel room — quite the unexpected move. I had a hunch about his intentions, which led me to reconsider my boundaries.

Pussy Policy #35: A woman gives her body when she loves, but a man gives his money when he loves. Focus on the treasury, not the physical activity.

Anyway, we went to see a movie that night. It was the weekend premiere of "Black Panther." I was incredibly excited to finally see the blockbuster. One thing I loved that we both had in common was our appreciation for Marvel movies. My entire family joined us that evening, both to get to know Michael better and to enjoy the film. It was an eventful occasion with attendees of all races donning African prints and brandishing the "Wakanda Forever" gesture. The movie symbolized hope for many of us, and I eagerly anticipated the creativity and the buzz surrounding it. That's where I was mentally: I cherished creativity and enjoyed stretching and flexing my mind to discover new ideas. As days passed, it became evident that Michael and I might not be as compatible as I'd hoped. This realization led me to establish another policy.

Pussy Policy #36: Don't commit to someone that you're not on the same frequency with as far as life goals, ambition, and leisure time. They will slow you down and hold you back from your true potential.

I sighed, acknowledging the truth I had been trying to ignore: it wouldn't last. Still, I decided to spend some time with him, treating it as if it had no consequence. I didn't see a long-term future with him; the attraction and mutual goals were lacking, but the intimacy was satisfying. You could say I was becoming addicted to the intimacy, though overall dissatisfied with the relationship. Hence, there was tension, but it eased up that particular day. He picked me up in his mom's Cadillac truck at seven-thirty sharp. He gazed at me as if I were a goddess but initially held back from commenting on my appearance. It felt as though he believed I was 'too good' for him or 'out of his league.' Yet, I loved him regardless. You see, women can develop love over time, and that's precisely what transpired with him. I didn't feel love at first, but with each date and shared experience, love gradually grew. He kissed me deeply after we stepped onto my mom's porch, out of her and Mason's view. My stomach fluttered from the experience. I was engulfed by the rush of adrenaline and the euphoria that came with it.

"You look good," he finally muttered after a few minutes.

"Thank you, sir," I said with a smirk.

"Are you ready to go?"

"Yes, of course I am. I have missed you," I said truthfully.

"I missed you too, babe."

It was moments like this… These moments gave me hope. These moments reassured me. These moments gave me love and affection, and that's really all I wanted and needed. For me, love was enough. Reciprocal love… Peaceful love…. And whole love. Love is the most beautiful gift on this planet. I needed it like I needed my next breath. I wanted it like a chocolate brownie doused in ice cream and fudge. It was a carnal desire, so I continued on that path to see where that story would lead.

We went to dinner and ate peacefully, initially.

"Why did you ask Gia why she chose Vince and not me?" he said with a pained expression.

'*Oh, shit,*' I thought. '*That damn Gia!*' Here we go!

"What are you talking about?" I said, trying to keep the irritation out of my voice.

"Gia said you asked her why she didn't choose me? Why ask that question?"

"It was a question that I had at that particular time," I said, unfazed by the new direction of the conversation.

"What was the goal there?"

"What is the goal here?" I said with growing agitation.

"I was just curious," he said.

"So was I," I said with amusement.

"You do know I was still with my ex at the time, right?"

"Of course, but I'm honestly not too convinced that men and women can be friends. Especially not when the man is straight, and the woman is attractive."

"Really. That's what you think?"

"So you never had feelings for Gia?"

"No, I've never had feelings for Gia. She was there when I went through a bad breakup. Nothing ever happened between us, and she found Vince around the same time. I was left single and alone, which led to me sleeping on their couch to cope with the pain of the breakup. It was the second time Rene had broken up with me, and it was starting to become a pattern. So, I decided not to beg her this time. I leaned on Gia for comfort to prevent myself from weakening and returning to Rene."

"Interesting," I said, sipping my amaretto sour.

"Why does all of that matter?"

"Because I need to know what I'm getting myself into."

"You mean, what you've gotten yourself into?" He smirked.

"Whatever."

"Gia is just like a little sister to me. Nothing more, nothing less."

"Whatever you say, chief," I said, needing to change the subject.

Note to self: Don't ask Gia shit else. She was his best friend, after all. We weren't cool like that anymore. Our friendship was a thing of the past, and I needed to start treating it as such. This was getting messy and had the potential of getting messier and exploding. Women are catty like that. Time to bow out gracefully. Well, as graceful as possible given this situation. Be cordial, not rude. Be pleasant, not mean. That was my goal from then on out.

We finished our dinner and focused on our enthusiasm for the upcoming movie. He had a surprise for me. I was enthusiastic about it. It was the one thing that seemed to lift my spirits after such an awkward conversation regarding Gia. See, I knew she would become a problem. I just didn't know how big of one as of yet. I swallowed that transgression and focused on enjoying my time with Michael. We saw the movie and met up with my family. They seemed to have liked Michael thus far.

"Hey, How are you doin?" my older brother asked Michael.

"Good, nice to see you again," Michael said to my brother emphatically.

He was such a stand-up guy. A good guy. I could look past his physical appearance if he continued to treat me well. The key word there was 'If."

My mother walked up to Michael and embraced him like he was her son. She seemed not to mind him. No, he wasn't a supermodel, but he treated me well for the most part. *Isn't that what mattered most?*

"That's some fine jewelry you have on Janeka. Let me borrow it for tomorrow," she said while sliding my jewels right off of me. I could not help but laugh because she couldn't wait until we got home. She knew I wasn't coming home, so she 'borrowed' my African pieces from me. I mean all of them. Michael laughed at the look on my face as she walked off with my jewels.

"Damn, your momma really shook you down," he laughed.

"Yeah, she did," I said, unfazed with humor in my voice. "Oh well. That's less I have to take off later."

"True," Michael said with a devilish look.

I rolled my eyes because I knew his mind was in the gutter. No worries. Mine was headed there later.

***

We arrived at the Westin Hotel in one of the most popular and expensive cities in Mississippi: Madison. I gawked at him in amazement. "What?" I exclaimed, looking at the hotel. He parked the car and went around to open my door. At least he was a gentleman on that front. I slid out of the car and looked up at him, the night's sky framing him, and smiled. "What are you planning?" I asked as his arms snaked around my waist. "A night to remember," he replied, smiling down at me knowingly. He certainly didn't disappoint in that department. I walked into the room; it was a suite. There was a bouquet of roses on the counter, a new pair of Nike shoes on the floor, chocolates on the bed, and a necklace from him in a little box. I was taken aback, realizing he had finally been paying attention to me. Perhaps things might look up after that night. Only time would tell. "Here, babe," he said, holding out a card for me. "Thank you so much," I replied, taking it and eagerly opening it to see his written words. But upon opening, it was just a generic 'Happy Valentine's Day' card with his name at the bottom. 'How generic,' I thought, disappointed. I had hoped for words of affirmation. No such luck there.

"What's wrong?" he asked.

"Nothing," I said, looking at the shoes down on the floor.

"Thank you so much," I said in appreciation that lacked real enthusiasm. It was progress, so I pushed my ungrateful thoughts and feelings back.

I focused on that night and enjoyed the quality time of the night. Of course, we had slow, passionate sex and just laid there enjoying each other's company. We were young, energetic, and free. Although he didn't have a real job, he did come through with this beautiful experience. I was thankful for it, sincerely. I fell even deeper. I wasn't sure if I wanted to end the relationship anymore. The intimacy was so intense, and the chemistry was so strong that I was second-guessing everything.

After that weekend, I was on cloud nine. I would daydream about him. I would dream about him. It was the dopamine rush. I was becoming 'addicted' to him, and I basked in the afterglow of our mating session. It felt so wrongfully sinful, but that was because it went directly against the values that I was raised with. This should have been reserved for my husband. I glanced down at him as he locked on to my left nipple and sucked gently until I got off on that act alone. I was very sensitive to touch, and I enjoyed his touch very much. It was feathery and gentle. Light and tender. It gave off the illusion of love, at least in that moment. I lay there and allowed myself to be penetrated as he broke down the defenses of my physical body and psychological space. It felt so good to be wanted. It felt even better being catered to. It was a privilege to touch me because I saw my body as a temple and a fortress. Everyone was not just walking in on their own accord. You had to be vetted. I didn't do a good enough job when it came to vetting Michael, and I knew it. I made a mental note to watch him closer for future reference. I chose to live for the moment, or at least for that moment.

***

The next day…

We were coming down from the high of the weekend. It felt wonderful. I felt thoroughly loved and entirely in love. It almost seemed too good to be true. I anticipated things would only get better, buoyed by the euphoria I felt. The relationship was beautiful. Yes, it had its ups and downs, testing all my fears, but it seemed worth the risks. After all, what's life without risks? Without them, we're not truly living; we're merely existing. That Sunday morning, we settled in at his parents' house, preparing for the upcoming Monday. I would have to return to my college campus an hour and a half away, while he remained in our hometown to finish his final semester. He sat next to me on his bed, opened his laptop, and I was left in sheer disbelief.

On that laptop was footage of us from the night before, and I was dumbfounded. Why would he film us without my consent? It was adding up.

"WHAT THE ACTUAL FUCK?" I exclaimed, sitting next to him. "Why did you film us?!!"

"Why not?" he said, as if that were normal. It wasn't, and I was totally turned off by it. It was so weird to me.

"Look, what is wrong with you? That is totally a violation of my privacy. Delete it now!"

"Ok. Ok," he said while appearing embarrassed.

"Why did you do that?" I said, honestly confused.

"It's something I've done in the past."

"I'm not your ex. That is totally unacceptable and a breach of trust," I said, bewildered. My mind was literally at a loss because of what he did. I was confused as to why he believed that to be ok. That was the most disrespected I've ever felt as a woman. That should have been the final tell-tale sign for me to hightail it out of that relationship, but sometimes we falsely believe we can change people. We can't. People are going to people. That's just the way it is.

Pussy Policy #37: Never allow someone to film you having sex; it could be held over your head.

"Look, I'll delete it. No problem. I'm sorry," he said, his face marked with embarrassment. "Don't ever do that again," I replied, my voice heavy with seriousness and concern. Hunter, the German Shepherd he once shared with his ex, chose that moment to let out a plaintive whine. I shot him a glance, and he fell silent. I watched Michael delete the video and decided I needed the rest of the day to myself to reflect on the entire situation. It was a huge turn-off. Yet, by then, I had developed a deep emotional connection, making it difficult for me to just walk away. Against my better judgment, I gave him another chance — the second time in that month. Deep down, I felt continuing was futile, but I pushed aside my intuition, overly concerned with what others might think, not realizing they had their own concerns. No relationship is perfect, but was this one worth the trouble?

Would this relationship be worth it in the long run? Would he change? Could he change? Did I even care if he did? Or was I merely seeking companionship, dreading the thought of loneliness? These were the tough questions I grappled with. What if there wasn't anything better out there for me? I had been single all my life and had finally let someone in. Could I move on now?

Pussy Policy #38: Never stay in a relationship that you're not sure of, especially if your gut tells you otherwise.

If I were being completely honest with myself, I would admit that my insecurities kept me entrenched in the relationship. I was overweight and believed I couldn't do better, that I didn't deserve better. Instead of addressing my insecurities, I remained complacent in the relationship. And guess what? My insecurities only intensified as I became more complacent and gained even more weight. In my mind, we were committed, so I felt no urgency to work out daily. He didn't make efforts to improve himself either.

He wore the same outfits nearly every day and had aged dreads that badly needed retwisting. He was complacent too. In his mind, he already had me; there was no need for self-improvement. It's curious how, sometimes, two individuals can regress in their health goals once they unite.

Pusssy Policy #39: Never let yourself go in a relationship; a relationship should make you better, not take you backward.

Chapter 15

GAME NIGHT

"The rich are not always wise, and the foolish are not always poor, but both play equal roles in the game of life until death comes to knockin' at all the doors."
~Sovereign Jane Jenkins

Jackson, Mississippi
February 23, 2018

A few weeks passed by, and the situation with the Valentine's Day massacre died down some.

Pussy Policy #40: Once you are disrespected on a major scale, leave, whether it's big lies, big deceptions, cheating, emotional abuse, and/or physical abuse.

I knew I probably made the worst decision by staying after that incident. I knew better, but I didn't act on that knowledge. I should have left and never looked back. There was an ulterior motive for why I stayed…What was it? I'll explain in a moment. Maybe the truth was, I wasn't only in love with him. I was in love with her as well….

Game night continued with all the couples gathered around. Uno, Cards Against Humanity, and Dominoes were the games of choice among the six couples. The room buzzed with energy and enthusiasm.

"Y'all ever been so constipated that you damn near cry on the toilet?" Vince asked.

"Yeah, and you feel the tear roll down your cheek," Michael responded with a laugh.

I glanced at Michael with annoyance. After the entire ordeal, my interest in him had significantly waned. Yet there I was. Maybe it was my fear of being alone or perhaps willful ignorance. That's the right term: I chose ignorance, finding comfort in its bliss. At that moment, my gaze shifted across the room, meeting Gia's. She smirked, clearly amused by the ongoing conversation.

Men tend to be more logical, while women are often more emotional. That was the entire reason I was still there: I was emotionally invested in the situation. However, when emotions run high, logic tends to exit the scene. It felt as if my logical side was observing me from outside, judging my choices. I pushed that thought aside, re-focusing on the present.

"Janeka, what are you thinking about?" Gia asked, suddenly appearing in my peripheral vision.

"Oh, just pondering," I replied, feigning cheerfulness despite my growing frustration.

"Oh, well. We're having brunch next week. You and Michael are welcome to join."

There it was—my invitation hinged on Michael's participation. I didn't want a relationship predicated on such conditions. I stifled a sigh, keeping my eyes from betraying my true feelings.

"Oh, that sounds nice. I had plans for a family gathering, but I'm definitely open to your event. It sounds fun."

Gia's smile suggested she'd scored a point in some unspoken competition. I mentally shrugged, suspecting this was just a popularity game. Whoever curried her favor most effectively, it seemed, would win the 'brunch contest.' Ha!

"She's always dropping these baby pellets," Vince joked, referring to Gia, drawing laughter from the group.

Her face turned beet red, and I laughed out loud. Any time she's embarrassed, she turns red. I saw that hadn't changed.

"Hush," she said, laughing.

The rest of the group discussed problems with relationships, but I realized that Michael's and I's relationship was the freshest out of the group. That made me nervous because ours was most likely to fail. I didn't want us to fail. I wanted genuine love. I wanted genuine affection that wasn't dependent on what I could do, my connections, or the knowledge I could give. I wanted someone to love me for me. Could Michael be that person? I honestly did not know, but from what I saw thus far, he was failing in a couple of categories. However, we had a strong connection, so I did not really know what to do.

"Janeka! How do you feel about relationships and violence?" Gia asked.

It seemed like all eyes were on me at that moment.

"I think violence in relationships is unacceptable. If you're feeling violent, you need to leave."

All the women seemed to harbor mixed feelings about that comment. I surmised they might have experienced their fair share of violent confrontations in the past. Although such encounters are not uncommon these days, I sincerely hope I never face such a situation. I am more of a lover than a fighter. Being an empath, I wear my heart on my sleeve, so violence would devastate me. I witnessed it frequently during my childhood and am determined not to endure it as an adult.

"If a woman hits me, she has three chances to knock me out," Cypris remarked. "Because after that third hit, instincts kick in to defend myself, and she might end up unconscious."

I shot him a sidelong glance and then observed his wife, thinking, "Surely, he didn't just say that out loud." She listened intently to his statement, appearing to concur with his perspective.

'These people must be smoking crack,' I thought to myself.

There is no way a man will be comfortable enough even to make that kind of statement while I'm here because if a man ever raised a hand to me, I'm gone like the wind without question. If you're comfortable enough to say it, you may feel comfortable enough to do it. We're not getting there. Ever.

"A woman can't just attack a man and expect to have no consequences. We're not punching bags," Cypris said.

I agree with that statement. It wasn't a woman's place to abuse a man, but someone needs to leave if it's a hostile environment. We all have flaws, but putting your hands on someone is out of the question.

"Violence is never the answer," another one of the females said.

"Thank you," I thought to myself. *Someone has some sense, finally.*

Women are beautiful creatures: soft, warm, affectionate, and naturally nurturing. I can't respect a man who would disrespect a woman in such a manner. I can't respect a man who would cheat on his queen, nor can I respect one who would mentally or physically abuse a woman. Such behavior is incomprehensible to me. Having witnessed my mom endure such treatment, I am resolute in not tolerating it in my own household. In that moment, I looked at Michael, hoping he possessed genuine wisdom; otherwise, that would be my unequivocal exit sign.

"The main thing that's important to me is that my wife is happy," Cypris said, feeling the energy centering around the room.

Every woman in the room sighed heavily, knowing he was trying to say what we women wanted to hear. Placating us to the max didn't change the insult. Pacifying us was never the correct course of action. Yes, I agreed that no woman should treat a man like a punching bag, but hitting her back instead of walking away was less than manly. It was downright scary.

"People are entitled to their own beliefs, and if that's what works for y'all, to each his own, " Gia said, sitting across from everyone.

Thank God, Sis has some sense as well. I could tell she was perturbed by the statement that Cypris made.

"Love is a beautiful experience, but some things are unacceptable, like violence. It is never acceptable for a grown man to put his hands on a woman, and it is also not acceptable for a woman to put her hands on a man," I said with certainty and calm resolve. Michael seemed to agree with that statement. I sighed in relief.

The group settled into a calm banter, and everyone seemed to decompress from the prior conversation.

We played more games like Phase Ten, Mystery Games, and Charades. I won every game.

"Yes, I won," I said with excitement. I was used to winning. That was my thing.

People laughed, cheered, and complained about the game, but ultimately, everyone had a great time. There was food, happy spirits, and good people all around, so it seemed to be a great friend group to be around. Or that's what I thought.

***

The Next Day…

"She didn't need to be so 'braggy'," Gia said to Michael the very next day through messages. See what I mean? Why did I feel like I needed to walk on eggshells around her? It was becoming ridiculous. This is why you can't have a girl best friend and a girlfriend at the same time. It gets messy quickly and unnecessarily. It felt like hazing, and I was growing tired of it. Gia was overstepping, and she needed to recognize her boundaries. If she didn't adjust her attitude towards me, a serious discussion or even an argument was imminent.

"Okay," Michael said over the phone. After ending the call with her, he turned to explain the situation to me.

"Gia mentioned you were being a bit too much at game night. Could you perhaps tone it down a bit?" he said, looking as perplexed as I felt.

"Are you serious?" I replied, unsurprised. My concern about my relationship with Gia was diminishing. I decided to prioritize my bond with Michael because, in the end, he was the reason I was there. I was dating him, not her. She shouldn't expect an apology; she might as well not hold her breath waiting for one.

"So, what do you want to do today?" I said happily, eager to change the subject from her.

"Well, Gia needs some help later on tonight with a chair, but we can do something before we head over to her house."

I rolled my eyes heavily.

"What? We just saw her yesterday," I said, growing increasingly uncomfortable with their relationship. They seemed too dependent on each other. It was unsettling. "I know, but we'll drop by for just a few minutes," he reassured, as if that settled the matter. "I just think we should focus on each other today," I countered, unconvinced. "Look, I don't know why you two aren't getting along. You used to be best friends." "Clearly, you can see it's not me." "Yeah, I can. I guess we'll figure it out as we go." "There's nothing to figure out. Clearly, she wants all your attention and nothing more." "I suppose," he said, scratching his head pensively.

"She introduced us. I thought it would be perfect. We're together because of her, after all."

I shrugged silently, knowing the intricacies of female friendships. It didn't mean much to me, as I was already over her, but I'd play along for his sake.

"How about this... I'll take you out on the town. We'll have a nice dinner, just the two of us. How does that sound?" he proposed, sitting in his chair opposite me as I remained on the bed. Although I was frustrated with Gia, I couldn't help but appreciate the effort Michael was making. I've always loved spontaneous, well-thought-out dates. They provide that dopamine rush. I love the idea and feeling of love. It's essential to me, like sunshine or nourishing soil. But being a hopeless romantic, I'm also vulnerable to potential mistreatment, so I always have to guard my heart and energy.

"Can we go to our special place?" I asked, planting a kiss on his lips.

"Of course," he replied in an animated voice. I was giddy with excitement and had high expectations. I had warned him many times before. Maybe he'd finally taken it to heart. When you love someone, you naturally want to see the best in them. It becomes challenging to let them go, especially if you've felt a lack of love in the past, like from a distant father. Such experiences can lead you to seek love in the wrong places. The key is to make choices not solely based on emotions. It's vital to master your feelings.

Pussy Policy #41: As a woman, never let your emotions overpower your intelligence.

"Alright, alright," I conceded, agreeing to visit Gia's after our date. Nothing, not even her, would ruin my day or evening. It was going to be wonderful, and the promise of intimacy added a cherry on top.

He beamed at me, a look of triumph in his eyes. In return, I smiled, resolved not to be affected by Gia's antics anymore. From now on, I would leave it to him to handle her. I had reduced my interactions with her to almost nothing, rarely texting her.

"Good," he remarked, leaning in to plant one last kiss on my lips before attending to something his mother had asked him to do earlier. Hunter, the dog he'd once shared with his ex, gazed up at me. He was a lovely pet, but to me, he still carried the baggage of Michael's past. He looked at me with pure innocence. Rising from the bed, I bent down to pet him.

"Hey, Hunter," I greeted. The German shepherd responded by affectionately licking my hand. Despite his association with the past, I found myself growing fond of him.

After another gentle lick, Hunter rested his head, embodying the typical laid-back canine demeanor. He reminded me a bit of myself – contemplative and quiet. I smiled at the realization, stood up, and caught my reflection in the mirror. Physically, I wasn't where I wanted to be, a personal insecurity of mine. Part of me wondered if I'd ever find someone better than Michael. Despite my reservations, I stayed, hoping he'd evolve.

While lounging on his bed, my gaze shifted to his phone on the nightstand. An impulse nudged me to sift through it. Taking it in my hands, I rationalized that if he hadn't wanted me to access it, he wouldn't have shared his password. Driven by curiosity, I navigated to his messages with Gia, eager to uncover their exchanges.

Him: What do you mean? What did Janeka do?
Gia: She didn't need to brag about winning every single game.
Him: I didn't really hear her brag too much, but I don't like that she undermines me and brushes me off from time to time. She doesn't like to listen to me.
Gia: Yeah, that's a problem.

Him: I know, and it's starting to puddle, and I need to mop it up, sooner or later, before it gets out of hand.
Gia: Definitely, before it gets out of hand....

I dropped the phone on his bed and rolled my eyes. This was some world-class nonsense. Sure, I'm not perfect, but I'm no villain either. It seems that when you enter a relationship, people constantly try to pigeonhole you, expecting you to conform to their idea of who you should be.

I live by my rules and at my pace, and they both could take a long walk off a short pier for all I cared. Frustration consumed me, and I felt myself withdrawing. It was as though I was seeking approval from some unseen tribunal. I knew this couldn't last. I sensed this relationship wouldn't endure the test of time. The warning signs were appearing too rapidly for me to even keep up. I felt restricted, unable to be myself, despite my usually strong sense of identity. The real question was, who did they think they were?

***

As I prepared for our date that night, I realized how much more comfortable I felt in black. It was due to the extra weight gain. While that was a personal insecurity, it wasn't his responsibility to reassure me. It was up to me to evolve into the best version of myself. Yet, there was a part of me that wanted to remain complacent, believing I had found my partner in him.

Our dinner was wonderful. We sampled drinks we'd never tasted before, and the food was exceptional. My hair was neatly braided into a simple ponytail, and I wore minimal makeup. I felt at ease in my skin around him, which meant the world to me.

Mid-meal, I posed a question. "What do you envision for yourself in the next five years?"

"I'd like to own businesses. Maybe even sell Great Danes…"

"Oh, hell no!" I burst out laughing.

"What! Is that a bad idea in your eyes?" he queried.

"Yes! First and foremost, who's going to deal with all that poop and pee?" I retorted.

"Well, that would be me. But consider the return on investment..."

"Yeah… No!" I chuckled. His expression showed a hint of disappointment. "Try again, honey," I said, still laughing.

"Well, what would you want to do as a hobby that makes money?" he said, prying for my future plans.

"I would be an author. I've always wanted to be a writer to inspire and entertain the world…." I said, feeling like a failure because I had yet to finish one book.

"Can I ask you something? Why did you name your build-a-bear Gia?" he asked with a straight face, suddenly changing the direction of the conversation.

I looked at him for a moment before responding. I had to think about that question because I really still didn't have an honest answer, but I had to give it my best shot.

"I like the name Gia," I said.

"That's it? Why not your third best friend's name?" he asked, referring to Amber. I felt like I was on the hot seat.

"Because I never heard of a name like 'Gia.'"

"So, you don't have feelings for her?"

I swallowed hard, thinking to myself deeper about the question.

"Why are you asking me that?"

"I'm trying to figure out why you and Gia have so much tension between the two of you."

" I don't know," I said, looking around the restaurant. The liquor had started to set in, and he knew it.

"Once upon a time, I had a crush on her, but that was years ago. I don't feel anything for her today."

"Ok," he said, sipping on his sweet tea.

***

Later that night…

Michael went ahead of me up the steps to Gia's house. I was using him as a human shield from her constant criticism. I wanted to be in and out. The less time I spent around her, the better, especially after the conversation I had just had with Michael.

He opened her front door, and I followed him in. I hoped that this time Gia wouldn't have a black eye.

"Hey, guys!" she greeted cheerfully, emerging from her bedroom.

Here come the theatrics, I thought to myself.

"Hey, Gia!" Michael responded.

"Hey," I replied with a flat tone, my tipsiness affecting my mood. It was hard to fake enthusiasm, especially with the influence of alcohol.

"How are you guys doing today?" Gia asked, settling onto the couch.

At least she didn't have a black eye this time, saving me from throwing suspicious glances at Vince again. The idea of women being abused didn't sit right with me.

I sat down, clearly irritated to be there in the first place. I should've been enjoying quality time with Michael. He'd hear about my feelings later, and I was sure our discussion would be... intimate. I found a smile creeping onto my face with that thought.

"What did you guys do today?" Gia inquired.

"It was date night... so, it was a good one," I responded, slightly emphasizing to throw a little shade her way.

Unfazed, she smoothly navigated the conversation, every bit the professional hotel receptionist and pre-med student she was. She was indeed skilled.

"So, guess who I talked to the other day?" she said, looking my way.

"Who?"

"Amber. She said she wants to get together with us, and we all catch up."

"Hmm. That's an interesting idea," I said, not caring for the camaraderie due to how it turned out with Gia.

"That's what I thought!" she said with a smile, reading me completely.

Michael looked at both of us with a goofy grin, too. They were literally the same person. He was essentially the male version of her. Maybe that's why I fell for him. Maybe that's why they clicked so well, besides her cattiness.

I sighed at the thought.

"Yes, y'all could do girly shit while I'm working next week," he suggested.

I could tell he really wanted us to get along.

So, for him, I gave it a try.

"Alright. That sounds good to me," I said, faking cheerfulness.

"Yay!" Gia jumped up from the coach, excited. She walked into the kitchen to fix something as if she were floating from the good news.

I was still skeptical of her intentions. She and Michael chatted while I scrolled through my phone on the far corner of the couch.

Then Vince walked into the front door.

Great, it's a party, I thought to myself.

"Hey, Vince!" I said calmly.

"Hey, y'all!" he says, coming in from work.

I wondered if he truly trusted Michael around Gia in his absence. He seemed unbothered by it. I could use a bit of whatever he was on because, to be completely honest, I viewed both of them with suspicion. I didn't like to share, and that was that.

Vince put his things away in his room and returned to the living room, turning on whatever sports were currently playing. Gia and Michael entered the living room and settled down with some snacks.

"So, what are you guys doing for graduation celebrations?" Gia asked.

"I have no clue what my mom has planned. Knowing her, half of my family will be there," I said.

"That's understandable. My family will be deep off in there too!" said Gia happily.

She has six brothers and sisters, so that was a very true statement; I couldn't imagine growing up in her household. Maybe that's why she was the way she was. Growing up, she wasn't the center of attention, so now she craves it or even demands it as an adult. That made perfect sense to me. Even though she treated me poorly as a 'friend,' I still felt some sort of empathy towards her. She didn't seem sad about the situation from her past. Maybe she found peace in her guy. He was her saving grace. That's why she always spoke highly of him. She gave him that praise that was due because, in a way, he saved her. Saved her from the home she considered hell due to her stepdad.

"You don't know what it was like growing up in a single-parent home," Gia said to Michael.

My ears perked up at the turn of the entire conversation.

'How did we get here?' I thought to myself.

"Yeah, it wasn't easy. I haven't seen my real father in over 20 years," Vince said solemnly.

"Yeah, I haven't seen mine in nearly two years," I said, feeling the heaviness in the room.

Michael became silent because, in truth, he really couldn't relate. He didn't know what a struggle it was growing up in a single-parent household. His struggle resided in the fact that he was insecure about his looks. He wasn't confident about himself. His self-esteem wasn't the best. I could tell he had been bullied and traumatized growing up. I didn't know how deep his wounds were, but I would stick around to find out and try to heal his traumas. It really wasn't my place, but I loved him.

Pussy Policy # 42: Never make a man that has not made you a wife a priority in regard to his traumas. It's his job to heal himself. Not yours. Stop trying to find projects to keep you distracted from your own ambitions.

For some reason, I thought of what Maria Theresa, Archduchess of Austria, did with her husband Franz Stephan. They're buried side by side in a double sarcophagus. Maria Theresa, Archduchess of Austria, did with her husband Franz Stephan. They're buried side by side in a double sarcophagus. Despite his infidelity, she remained dedicated to him after his passing. While I wouldn't tolerate cheating, the theme of unwavering commitment to my spouse would be the guiding force in my life. If Michael wasn't the one for me, I prayed for God to reveal it soon. Perhaps He already had, and I had missed the signs. Nevertheless, I remained, eager to see where love would lead.

I remembered the first time we watched a movie at his house. We sneakily got intimate while his parents were asleep in the front room. Looking up at him, I remarked, "You are so adorable with your fine self." He recoiled as if I'd slapped him. I realized that calling him 'fine' was as traumatizing to him as using the 'N' word. I resolved never to use either term.

I snapped back to the present conversation, my smile tinged with sadness. The atmosphere was heavy, with everyone reflecting on their pasts, careful not to delve too deep into their traumas. Such journeys weren't always safe. Trauma was the word of the day, the byproduct of having a father who chose to leave. That was the consequence. Michael would never truly understand. It wasn't my job to make him, but I sought acceptance. Acceptance of my flaws, including perhaps not fully valuing his presence, might emerge as issues later on. Regardless, I was committed, and I wanted him to know that.

"Yet, not having him in my life made me stronger. I can proudly say I never needed him. I succeeded in spite of that bastard," Vince declared.

His words struck a chord within me. We shared that experience, and I started to understand Vince on a deeper level. Gia seemed uneasy, perhaps noticing the pain Vince tried to hide. This topic resonated with all of us in different ways.

"I can't relate to not having my father around," Michael admitted. "But life wasn't always easy, even in a two-parent household."

"What's easy in any relationship?" I quipped at Michael. "All we're saying is you had experiences we couldn't share. I didn't find out who my real father was until I was twelve. Can you imagine the trauma that inflicts on a young girl? Abandonment, attachment, trust issues... the list goes on." I glanced at Gia as I spoke, realizing neither she nor Vince could truly understand that particular pain. Among us, I was the only one raised in such circumstances.

'Lucky y'all,' I thought to myself.

"Ok. Ok. Got it," Michael said, preferring to change the subject at that moment, opting out of the silent "who had it worse" competition.

"So, do y'all want to play a game?" Michael asked.

"What kind of game?" Gia asked.

"Any kind," Michael said.

"I have this game for couples that I just downloaded. We can try that out," Gia said.

"Ok," I said, relieved for the distraction from my past memories beginning to flood my mind.

Gia sat on the couch across from Michael and me while Vince sat in a single chair to my right.

"Reenact a strong orgasm," Gia said, laughing.

'Oh, it was one of those games,' I laughed silently to myself. *I was going to win this!*

"No, I can't do that," said Gia laughingly. She picked up the tequila shot because she did not complete the dare.

It was Vince's turn next.

"Lick whip cream off of Gia's neck," Vince's dare read.

I laughed because that was very appropriate.

He looked at Gia and shrugged like it was nothing.

"We don't have any whipped cream, but this honey will do," he said, standing and grabbing the honey off the table. He walked over to the couch, and Gia giggled and obliged and scooted to the edge of the couch to accommodate him. He poured a few drips on her neck; Michael and I laughed at the lightness of the gesture. He slowly licked the honey off her skin while she laughed. After completing the deed, he returned to his seat and sat down with a devilish grin.

I knew what they were going to be doing later…

"Alright, Neka. It's your turn."

"Re-enact doggy style with Michael," I said, laughing and embarrassed.

"You going to do it?" Gia taunted.

"Hell, yeah! I'm not a punk!" I boldly stated, getting to my hands and knees on the carpet. Gia and Vince laughed hysterically as Michael got behind me, goofily laughing at this situation. Michael and I sat back on the couch afterward. My face was beet red, but it was a relief after the prior conversation. The room was light again. The game continued. It was my turn once again.

"Janeka, sexually lick Vince's neck," I said, looking at Michael with a skeptical look.

Michael shrugged.

"It's just his neck," Gia laughed.

"I don't think that's a good idea. I sweat back there," Vince said.

Vince was the oldest in the group. He was the only person over 30 years old. He knew the deeper indications of opening that kind of door more than we understood at the time. Humans are human, and people are people. One thing people are going to do is fall victim to temptation. Vince didn't even want to touch that with a long-handled spoon, and I respected that.

"Gia, do you want to be my fill-in?" I said, relieved that Vince made that statement.

"Sure!" She popped up from the couch and licked Vince on his neck.

I was still lightheartedly laughing that we even were playing this game.

"This game is for singles," Vince said, laughing at what the rest of us believed to be true.

"Tongue kiss Gia," Michael's dare read.

I could feel my left eye twitch at that dare. THAT WASN'T HAPPENING.

"I tag in Janeka," Michael said.

My eyebrow twitched just then, and I was stunned. Surely, Gia was going to say no to that. She literally couldn't stand me.

"Ok. Are we doing this, Janeka? I'm in," Gia said.

"Ok," I said, sliding off the couch.

"Let's go brush our teeth," Gia said.

We both went into the bathroom to brush our teeth. She passed me an unused toothbrush, and we both brushed our teeth side by side in the mirror. It's funny because I wasn't expecting anything more than a peck on the lips. We both then returned to the living room after brushing liberally. I had mixed feelings about it, but it was a game. What's the worst that could happen?

Michael nor Vince seemed to be too bothered by it, but I wasn't really paying attention to them. I was in my head for the most part. I sat back on the couch next to Michael, not knowing what else to really do with myself. Gia got on my lap, and we kissed. It was intimate. It was sweet. It was surprisingly passionate and lasted longer than necessary. It made me hot and bothered, which shocked me because I didn't realize the implications of such a simple act. It wasn't simple at all. It was Pandora's box. The door to the box was now open, and I couldn't stop the assault of dirty thoughts and raging hormones flooding the gates of my mind.

I heard Michael audibly gasp while sitting next to me. I had no clue what Vince's face looked like, but I was grossly occupied at the time, so I couldn't look his way. I guess the passion was just that palpable.

Gia broke the kiss and hopped up abruptly.

"That was great, but my baby kisses better," she sing-songed.

I was dumbfounded.

"I'm sure," I said languidly. I looked at Michael, and he had this funny look on his face. I looked at Vince, and he had a suspicious look on his face. It was something like I was infringing on his property. I backed up with my hands up in my mind.

'Rest assured. This can't go anywhere, big fella.' I thought to myself. *I'm not trying to take your girl.*

Chapter 16

THE AFTERMATH

Love is beautiful.
Love is sweet.
Love is everything that I need.
Love touches the heart.
Some things hurt without a warning or 'nothin'
Never in this life would I have thought that I would love a woman.
~Sovereign Jane Jenkins

Jackson, Mississippi
February 27, 2018

The cruelest thing about love is that it doesn't always love you back, and sometimes you don't realize this fact until it's too late and your heart has thawed and has become puddy in someone else's hands.

I sat there in Michael's bed, daydreaming about Gia. It was the curse of a lifetime. Everything I thought I felt for her in the past returned with a vengeance. It was almost comical that everything was unfolding, but what should a girl do? I looked to my left and saw Hunter looking at me looking at him.

"What?" I said. "I don't know what life is either."

He put his head down on the new bed I bought him for Christmas. I smirked because he seemed to enjoy the bed genuinely. It was a nice gesture to prove that I didn't hate him. He was actually pretty sweet and made good use of it. He was calm, and it was good for my spirit.

"Have you ever been in love with two people?" I asked him.

He looked at me again, and his right eyebrow curled up.

'I guess not,' I thought to myself.

That kiss should not have happened. It's like it lit my soul on fire. Surely, that wasn't normal. Was it?

Michael walked back into the room, holding his plate of chicken.

"And you don't have feelings for Gia?" he asked for the 3rd time that day.

I looked up at him and felt like I couldn't admit it out loud. It would make it too real. Too personal. Too honest.

"It was one kiss. That's it," I said, unwilling to admit the truth out loud.

"It was one kiss that was way too passionate to ignore," he said good-naturedly.

"Whatever…" I said, ignoring and purposefully dodging the question.

He sat down with his plate and handed me mine. We ate in silence and watched the movie. The food was amazing. His mom could really burn.

"What do you think about taking a trip with them?"

"It could go well," I said thoughtfully.

"I'll see what Gia says."

"It's all Gia. Why did you tag me yesterday?"

"I know you have feelings for her."

"Ok. You're comfortable with that?"

"Vince is not about to let her go, so I'm not worried."

"I'm only focused on my own home."

"Oh, really?" he said with love in his eyes.

I realized I must've said the right thing because the next thing I knew, lips were headed my way.

"That was such a sweet thing to say," he said while kissing me.

"I mean it," I said between kisses.

He pulled back and stared at me for a few minutes.

"I love you," he said.

"I love you too," I said.

I felt complete at that moment. Maybe it was because I finally found a love of my own. I needed that. That's what I craved my entire life. I just wanted love. Healthy love was my priority. That's it. I was a simple yet complex woman. I was easy to please but complex to understand, like most women. I appreciated the experience with Michael, even if it didn't last long term. I was a better person in this relationship. Maybe not physically, but emotionally. I had gained a few pounds of love weight and was happy. I was genuinely happy and in love. It didn't get much better than that, did it? That's all I truly wanted.

I took a step back and analyzed the moment. He accepted me for who I was and where I was, and I decided right then that I'd do the same for him.

"Baby, where do you see us in five years?" I said.

"I don't know. Maybe Texas? Or can we go to Georgia? Or we can go to California? I don't want to stay in Mississippi."

"I don't want to stay here either."

"Good, we're on the same page."

"Absolutely," I said.

"Why did you choose me?"

"Because you were you. You gave me your shoes," I said honestly.

He smirked, kissed me on my forehead again, and hugged me from the side.

He smelled good.

"You smell like Michael," I said.

He laughed and looked down at me and said, "What?"

I was addicted to his smell. The oxytocin rush. The dopamine feeling. It was all hitting me at once, and I forgot my feelings for Gia. This was love. Or it felt like something very close to it. Maybe it was finally trusting someone outside of my family. I needed to believe in mankind again, and I realized then that Michael was helping me get over that trauma.

Maybe my momma was wrong. Maybe it could work. Time will tell.

"You're not the only one that has a past, Janeka. We all have something that we are ashamed of. We all have a past. I am ashamed of something I did as a young teenager," he said honestly.

"What is your shame?" I asked thoughtfully.

"I can't tell you," he said. I felt deflated. I poured my heart out to him, but he was holding back.

"What is your shame?" I asked curiously.

"It's not important," he said.

"You said that you love me and that you want to marry me, but you can't tell me about your shame?"

"No, it's not important."

"But if it's important enough for you to bring up in conversation, then it does matter. If it didn't matter, then you would've kept it to yourself. Does Gia know about it?"

"No, she does not. It's really bad," he said sadly.

"What is it? I won't tell a soul," I said honestly.

"When I was a teenager, I had sex with my neighbor's female dog," he said, looking down at his feet.

My stomach dropped into my shoe as I blinked at him for a few minutes in silence and tried to fix my face. I wasn't sure what to say. That was simply way out of my scope of practice. I wasn't a therapist or a psychologist, but maybe he should consider seeing someone since that happened when he was young. It demonstrated a lack of self-control at a very young age, which worried me. Beastiality is considered a sickness, so I thought he should talk to a professional about that. What would happen if we had a child? Would he touch his own child? So many things assaulted my psyche that I became dizzy from the stream of thoughts. *What do you even say to a person who said something like this out loud?*

So I said nothing. Nothing at all. I just stared at him with a worried look. I mean, he was a teenager, sure. However, how much lack of self-control does a man have over his penis? *Would he cheat on me once we were married? Would he touch our children?!!*

So many terrifying thoughts ran through my head as he suddenly shifted the direction of the conversation.

"You know, you're very tight. Maybe it's because you're 'short,'" He said, knowing that I hate hearing the 's' word. I wasn't ashamed of being short, but he made it known that it was a drawback for him. I guess fucking dogs was a drawback for me, but I'd be wrong if I said that out loud, wouldn't I? I cleared my throat audibly instead and swallowed my rebuttal.

"What does that have to do with the price of pussy in China?" I asked with an attitude.

"Nothing. I was just pointing out that compared to my ex, you're very tight. She was more on the loose side. She wasn't a virgin when we met, though," he continued to ramble.

"Ok..," I said flatly while staring at him strangely.

"I heard Rene had a boyfriend. So, it's cool for us to be friends, right?" he said while sitting on the side of the bed, trying again and successfully shifting the subject.

My head snapped in his direction so fast that I nearly gave myself whiplash.

"No, the hell it isn't. How do you know she has a boyfriend?" I said, staring at him as if he had two heads. He looked taken aback at that line of questioning.

"We were together for a long time. It's not easy just letting go, and I saw it on social media," he said emphatically.

"Listen… I said it before; I'll say it again. It's either her or me. You choose. Because if you can't let her go, I'm going," I said, putting my perpetual foot down.

Pussy Policy #43: If you give an ultimatum, be ready to fulfill the follow-through.

"Ok," he said.

"Ok, what?" I asked.

"I'll eventually let it go altogether."

"What does that even mean?" I said, daring him to continue.

"I'll let her go," he finally said, getting it right.

I shouldn't have to keep repeating myself. This was unacceptable. Honestly, I knew he wasn't over her, but I'll be damned if I just wasted my virginity on this man for nothing. That would be a huge joke on me, and I damned sure wasn't laughing. I was offended.

Pussy Policy #44: Never stay with a man that is still in contact with his ex; he needs to be free and clear for a good six months after a long-term relationship before dating him.

"I don't want to hear about her again!"

"Ok," he said with a look of defeat.

Pussy Policy 45: Don't feel guilty for setting stringent boundaries.

Looking back, this was a significant red flag, one among the myriad others I had chosen to overlook. I know — I should have walked away at the first sign of trouble, right? I deserved better, didn't I? Of course, I did. But I didn't believe I did. The nagging question, 'What if I couldn't find anything better?' always loomed. He had such a strong attachment to her. I've noticed that men often struggle with closing doors completely. I should have left the moment he suggested they remain friends. But the powerful cocktail of emotions, perhaps driven by dopamine, oxytocin, and serotonin, kept me anchored. The entanglement with Gia only made matters murkier.

After finishing my chicken, my appetite was ruined, and the weight of our repeated conversations about this issue made me need a break from him. If he truly wanted her, he should just go to her and leave me out of it. His audacity to ask such a thing was astounding, because had our roles been reversed, we wouldn't be having this conversation. I took one more look around his room, noting again that he still lived with his parents. The audacity of it all was staggering.

Pussy Policy #46: Never date a man that doesn't have his own house, car, or job if you yourself have all three; those are the big three.

Bonus Rule~

Pussy Policy #47: Match the energy of the person you're with and just sit back and be attentive.

Sometimes, people don't appreciate you until you're gone out of their lives. That's just the way it is. It's the cruel reality of living the gift of life, but living is still a beautiful experience. For some reason, I couldn't break free from him right away, and not because I did not want to, but because I was curious about what that kiss was about between Gia and me. Maybe it was just high hormones from the drinking games. Or maybe it was just the beginning of another soul tie/attachment. I didn't like attachments at all; they made things confusing and messy. I was starting to regret that kiss because it made things grossly complicated. I was heterosexual, after all. I craved sex from my boyfriend, not anyone else. That was the one thing he always got right. He always touched the right spots and rubbed me in the right places. It was addictive, and I was starting to understand why a healthy sex life was important. However, this started to feel more like quicksand. You fall in love quickly, but it's hard as hell getting out of the situation. I would be way more comfortable if I was married. I couldn't fully drop my guard for him because we could break up anytime, and he would be moving on to another woman. The thought bothered me because that meant that the last few months would have been a complete waste of time. I didn't like wasting my time, so "What's a girl to do?"

***

Michael and I had been officially dating for five months. We communicated every day, and he was consistently attentive. However, on this particular day, two whole hours passed since I woke up, and there was no message from him — quite out of character. It was rare for me to initiate conversations. Typically, he would reach out the moment he woke, especially on Mondays. Puzzled, I headed to the bathroom in my dorm. Staring into the mirror, I saw my reflection: attractive, yes, but not content. The weight gain was really getting to me. — a side effect of "love," perhaps? I focused on my stomach, where I primarily gained weight, and sighed. *Will I ever shed these pounds?* This relationship seemed to be slowing down my progress, and I felt I couldn't take the initiative since I believed in following Michael's lead. Maybe we could eventually motivate each other.

My mother always advised, "Mirror the men but set the relationship's tone. How you begin determines its course." Maybe she had a point. Perhaps I needed to be more assertive with Michael about my expectations. I'd told him repeatedly that I appreciated gifts — tokens that showed he thought of me outside our meetings. Yet, more often than not, he arrived empty-handed. I tried to lead by example, buying his favorite snacks and showing thoughtfulness, but my gestures were seldom returned. At least he was covering most of our meals now. That was one less thing to contend with. Dining alone was preferable to dealing with a stingy partner. I was relatively new to relationships, but an instinct told me I might be settling for less than I deserved.

Pussy Policy #48: Don't give your everything to someone that has given you nothing. A man has done nothing until he has given you a ring and taken you as a fiancé or wife.

I left the bathroom a few minutes later, hearing my phone go off—finally, a text from Michael.

Him: Hey, Good afternoon.
Me: Hey, are you ok?
Him: I didn't have the best day. I have something to tell you.

I balked, thinking what it could have been that would cause him to have a bad day and text me later than usual.

Him: I failed my Statistics test.

Me: ok.

I had taken statistics a year and a half prior, so I was used to that kind of news from that course. However, I passed it with an 'A'.

Me: Don't let that get you down and ruin your day!
Him: No, you don't understand. I failed the class and won't be able to pull the grade back up.
Me: Ok…..
Him: That means that I won't be able to graduate on time.

My stomach sank at the news. Graduation was only two months away. While I was on track to earn my Bachelor of Science in Nursing, he had been on course for his Bachelor of Science in Computer Engineering. Yet, that path was now disrupted by a single class. I couldn't help but laugh at the irony.

Unsure of how to respond, I chose not to reply to his message. As expected, he called after just five minutes. Sitting at my desk, I was engrossed in studying for my upcoming exam in Complex. I didn't have the luxury of time to console him. The principle was simple: if at first you don't succeed, try again. It seemed his graduation would now be in December. Had I been a distraction? Perhaps. However, I wasn't going to find myself in the same predicament. I had already postponed my graduation by a semester to minor in Spanish. Further delays weren't an option for me; it was time to move forward. Lost in thought, I missed his call. Predictably, he called back, and I could sense the growing panic in his actions.

"Hey," I said in a cheery tone—no need to be morbid. No one died here.

"Hey, babe. I'm so sorry that I didn't text you this morning," he said, sounding exacerbated by his current circumstances.

"I am just at a loss for words right now," he said, sounding upset at the situation.

"What happened?" I said curiously.

"The professor was from India, and he was very difficult to understand, and I didn't pass the last exam because of it."

I immediately realized that he wasn't taking responsibility for his life. The teacher could have been hard to understand, but he had notes, textbooks, and good ole Google as resources.

"So….. What are you going to do?" I said, testing his problem-solving abilities.

"I'm going to drop the class," he said sadly.

"Good, then make sure you pass the rest of your classes," I said stoically.

From what I knew of him, he was at best a 'C' student. He spent most of his time gaming, goofing off, or immersed in relationships, never truly realizing his potential or discovering who he was as a man. It wasn't my job to shape him. He had to figure that out on his own.

"Alright, I have to study, so I'll talk to you later," I said, eager to end the call.

I could almost hear his thoughts: 'She's going to break up with me.'

I wasn't about to stay on the phone and counter that assumption. After all, I might just consider it. I've always been hesitant, one foot in and one foot out of the relationship. Much depended on how he navigated this present challenge. I settled at my dorm room desk to work on my thesis. As a member of the Honors College, I was determined to graduate with the esteemed Magna Cum Laude distinction. My research focused on the impact of hypermasculinity on African-American males in nursing. As I typed, my thoughts raced at an unparalleled pace.

Chad: Hey, beautiful!

I looked down at my phone. Should I answer this message? Is it cheating? Is it wrong? Probably so, but Michael was still in contact with his ex, so…

Messages:

Me: Hey, guy!
Chad: What have you been up to?
Me: Just studying for finals. You?
Chad: Just sitting here in the library thinking about you.
Me: Oh, really? Happy thoughts, I hope.
Chad: Why do you think I texted you?
Me: Hmm…To procrastinate.
Chad: I don't do much of that. I get stuff done when needed.
Me: I heard that! How are your classes going?
Chad: Great! I'm about to Ace this biology test.

That's the type of news I wanted to hear. I sighed in guilt. Was I wrong? No. As the saying goes: 'All's fair in love and war.'

I chatted with Chad for a few minutes and glanced at the time. My complex class, the current bane of my existence, was about to start. I pondered whether I should lunch with Chad to get to know him better, but time would determine that decision. What would Gia think of Michael's current dilemma? I didn't plan on asking. The dynamic of our relationship felt one-sided. Why was I consistently the one initiating? Why was I always investing more effort? She spent more time reprimanding me than being a true friend. Hence, I pulled away. I wasn't going to force a connection. I wasn't infatuated with our past kiss anymore, either. Time has that effect. I recognize genuine love from mere tolerance.

My phone vibrated again; Michael was calling.

"Hey, what's up?" I inquired as I answered.

"Hey, babe. What are you doing?"

He probably sensed some mischief. Well, we weren't married; I had every right to explore my options.

"I'm about to head to class. Why?" I responded, gathering my essentials: laptop, snacks, and highlighters. I loved color-coordinating my notes with highlighters; nursing school demanded such organization.

"Oh, okay. Just checking in." I could hear his tone's underlying need for reassurance, but I wasn't in the mood to indulge it. I decided to divert the conversation.

"Thanks for that. I'm sending you a draft of my graduation invitation. What do you think of the color scheme?" I asked, sending the screenshot.

There was a pause after my message went through. He remained silent for a couple of minutes.

"Why's there so much on it?" he finally questioned.

Puzzled, I looked at the screenshot. "You mean my achievements over the last four years?"

"Yeah, it seems excessive. Perhaps you should remove some."

His words caught me off guard. Why would he suggest I diminish my hard-earned accolades?

"Why would I do that?" I queried, genuinely perplexed.

"It's just cluttered. Half of that stuff won't matter post-graduation," he stated bluntly.

"Excuse me!" My voice raised unintentionally in the cafeteria. "You have surely lost your mind," I retorted, feeling a surge of indignation.

Pussy Policy # 49: Never get with a man that diminishes your accomplishments, accolades, and goals.

"I'm just asking: what's the point of adding all that? You're already going to have a ton of sashes on graduation day," he said, a hint of bitterness and jealousy evident in his voice.

"Look, you won't dim my shine. If you can't handle my light, let me know now so we can end this without wasting any more time," I responded, keeping my tone even.

"Woah! Where is this coming from? I was just saying the card looked cluttered. Why are you getting so worked up?" he retorted, seeming genuinely puzzled as if he weren't trying to undermine my accomplishments.

"Because it's nonsense," I shot back. "You're essentially criticizing who I've become by making such a ridiculous statement."

"Really? Just because I suggested removing something from the card?" he asked, sounding offended.

Pussy Policy #50: Try not to date below your level; find someone on your level physically, spiritually, emotionally, and psychologically. When you date down, they try to pull you down with them.

The more I stuck around Michael, the more I could see that there were some major insecurities at play on his behalf.

"You know what? I'll talk to you later," I said, hanging up in his face.

I immediately called my mom to tell her about the exchange.

"Should I take something off the card, momma?" I said, picking her brain.

"Hell, Naw! Is that motherfucker crazy? You keep all that shit on there. That's four years of celebration for your accomplishments. Just because he's failing doesn't mean you are not going to shine."

"Yes, ma'am," I said.

"Are you sure about this relationship, Janeka?"

"No, ma'am. Not at all," I said on the verge of tears.

"Don't get in too deep."

"Yes, ma'am!" I said, knowing my mama was right.

My phone began to ring, indicating the other line was occupied.

"Hold on, mama. Let me call you back," I said, clicking over.

"What?" I said in an annoyed tone.

"I was just saying…. Why brag about all those things people won't remember?" he said sternly.

"I just got off the phone with my mother. You will never stop my shine. Leave me be if you can't be supportive and happy for me!"

"Ok," he said, realizing he had really stepped in it. "I'm sorry. Are you ok?" he asked.

"I'm fine. I'll call you back later," I said, ending the phone call. Was I wrong in the way in which I treated him? No, I wasn't. I could sense him trying to obtain more power and control over me. That simply would not do. I was not his momma nor his superwoman, nor was I his subordinate. He needed to figure life out for himself. I had enough issues to worry about.

I ran out of my room towards the nursing building. I had an extra pep in my step because I couldn't stay another semester to graduate. His situation lit a fire under my ass to pass my own classes.

Pussy Policy #51: Don't always try to fix someone else's problems; you may end up being used.

Chapter 17

'CUFFIN' THE SOUL

"Although I took my heart off my sleeve long ago, the tie that I can't see is slowly entwining itself in my soul."
~**Sovereign Jane Jenkins**

The next day…

As I was leaving my final class of the day, I looked over to the bulletin board and saw that the campus glow run was happening that upcoming Saturday. I was excited because I had forgotten all about it. I wondered if Michael wanted to come. Then, I paused in thought. We hit it off well in conversation, but I didn't want to go anywhere we could get made fun of. I mean, I was fat and overweight while he was tall, skinny, lanky, and was a five in the face. Superficial, I know; sadly, we live in a superficial world. That's just the way it is. However, I knew the race would help him to feel better and build some confidence within himself. So, I invited him anyway.

Me: Hey, babe! Would you like to run a Glow Run this weekend? It's three miles long.
Him: Hey, Janeka! Sure. It sounds fun.
Me: I hope your day is going well!
Him: It's ok.

I could tell he was still upset about the class, so I tried not to make a big deal out of it. As long as he graduated and remained on some kind of track, that became my mindset. After all, one slip-up on a test in nursing school could result in me graduating a semester later. I needed to stay humble regardless of the circumstances. If I were in his shoes, I'd also want someone to stick with me through thick and thin.

Messages:

Me: I love you.
Him: I love you too.

Gia: Hey, Neka! How are you?
Me: I'm good, and you?
Gia: Great! I was just checking on you. How are your classes going?

I blinked because that was outside of the normal status quo for her, at least when it came to me.

Me: Oh, ok.
Gia: Sooooo, you heard about the news from Michael? He's not graduating with us...

I rolled my eyes because she was only fishing. She wasn't genuinely interested in me. She was interested in how I was going to handle his situation. I wasn't. Plain and simple. I'm only watching from the sideline.

Pussy Policy #52: Never let another female see you sweat when it comes to any man.

Me: Uh, huh. I am aware.
Gia: How do you feel about it?
Me: I'm focusing on my classes. He'll figure it out.

Gia: But… Do you think you'll move back home after graduation?

I wondered if Michael put her on this line of questioning because this wasn't her business. I no longer trusted her on THAT level.

Me: I don't know. I'm only focused on graduating for now.
Gia: Ok, I understand. You definitely should. Things are getting real.
Me: They have been real for me. It might have just got real for Michael.
Gia: Well, if you need anything, let me know!

I laughed out loud at that statement. "Sure, girl, sure!" I thought to myself.

After walking across campus to the cafeteria for a few minutes, my phone began to ring.

I looked down, and it was Michael calling.

"Hey, babe!" I said in my best chipper voice, looking around to see if any cars were coming as I crossed the street.

"Hey, Janeka!" Michael practically screamed into the phone.

He sounded like he was in a rush.

"What's up?" I asked, slightly alarmed at his haste.

"I found out something today! I found out that one of my classes that I took at my previous community college could count towards graduation, and I won't need statistics after all," he rushed to say. I could tell he was damn near sprinting somewhere.

"Oh, that's awesome! That means we can all graduate on time!"

"Exactly! I'm headed to get my transcript from the community college now so I can take it into my college's administration building."

I was genuinely happy for him. I didn't know the type of disappointment he was feeling, but I did know that he sounded like he could rule the world now.

"Well, I'm here cheering you on!" I said, hoping that it wasn't going to be another disappointment.

"Thank you, babe! I will call you once I get everything in!" he finally said.

"Cool babe!"

"I love you!" he said before hanging up the phone.

I didn't get to say it back, so I figured he was riding a high of hope right about now. I'll leave him to it, then.

I walked into the cafeteria and grabbed the food that looked somewhat appetizing. I walked around the cafeteria until I saw Chad. He was sitting next to the window facing away from me.

I walked towards him, and I guess he could sense me walking from behind him because he turned around and stood up.

Pussy Policy #53: Until you're in a committed and faithful relationship, keep a pair and a spare. KEEP YOUR OPTIONS OPEN! Date everybody, but don't sleep with everybody.

My relationship with Michael continued to be rocky throughout that period. Consequently, I kept my options wide open. After all, he was still in touch with his ex, and I had a feeling it would only be a matter of time before she resurfaced. It had become an every two to three-month pattern. Two can play that game, but in the end, no one wins. If nothing changes, everyone stands to lose. Until then, what Michael didn't know...

"Hey, Beautiful!"

"Hey, Chad!" I said, giving him a brief hug.

"How are you feeling?"

"I'm feeling well. It's good to see you."

"It's good to see you as well."

I sat down in front of Chad and smiled.

"How's your classes?"

"It's good. Yours?"

"Great, as always!"

"Good," he said, grabbing my hand and kissing the back of it.

We chatted for an hour, and then he looked out of the window.

"Look," he said.

I looked, and there were two African American girls walking along the path outside, eating Chick-fil-A with their pudgy stomachs showing. They appeared to be in a rambunctious conversation that included expletives. A white girl was running by them at that same moment with a sports bra and leggings on.

"See that?" he said, still looking.

"I do," I said, still slightly confused as his point evaded me.

"The white girl is conscious and proactive about her health, while many of us in the black community hesitate to prioritize exercise but will rush to Chick-fil-A for a quick bite. People wonder why black individuals have higher rates of heart attacks and strokes compared to other races. It's because of such choices," he said, wearing a grave, disapproving expression. Chad was a deep thinker, which I admired. He made a valid point, which I appreciated too. Glancing down at my lunch—a salad, pizza, and some veggies—I realized I hadn't done too poorly, but he reminded me that I could always strive for better. I smiled at him as his focus shifted back to me.

"What are your health goals?" he asked.

"Lose fifty pounds."

"What's your timeframe?"

"I don't know yet."

"A real goal is definite," he said with a straight face.

I became uncomfortable because I realized with Chad, I might be biting off more than I was ready to chew, or maybe it was my insecurities. He was attractive, athletic, young, smart, and intuitive, but why couldn't I keep my mind off of Michael? A guilty feeling was gnawing in the pit of my stomach. I loved Michael, that's why. Or that's what I told myself to battle my insecurities because I felt Chad was a little out of my league.

***

That Next Saturday…

Michael was driving up to the school for the Glow Run, and my nerves were frayed. He had never accompanied me to a public college event where he'd meet all my friends; the thought of it made me uneasy. I couldn't understand my own feelings. Sure, he was just a person, but part of me didn't want to be seen with him. Why did I feel this way? My anxiety heightened as the minutes passed. I occasionally suffered panic attacks, often triggered by the pressures of nursing school. I glanced at the anxiety medicine I kept nearby. Taking it would leave me groggy for two days. My panic intensified. The troubling thoughts overwhelmed me: What if people ridiculed him? Would I end up defending the man I loved? The guilt of having these thoughts weighed heavily on me. Was it a matter of physical compatibility? Would I even have these doubts if we looked "better" together? I was overwhelmed with uncertainty.

My phone rang. Predictably, it was Michael. Perhaps he was waiting outside. Paralyzed by anxiety, I let it ring. I hoped he might reconsider attending the run. But then my phone rang again. Staring at the screen, I felt wholly unprepared for the evening. Eventually, I mustered the courage to approach my desk and answer.

"Hello," I said with a shaky voice.

"Hey, babe! Are you ok?"

"Yeah, I guess. Just a little anxious."

"You need me to bring you something?"

"No! I'm fine."

"Cool, then I'm outside," he said.

My eyebrows furrowed, suspecting that he had once again shown up empty-handed. I had made my expectations clear: I valued gifts, as they were my love language.

Lost in these thoughts, I walked outside to greet him. I opened the door, and there he was, standing empty-handed, waiting expectantly. Approaching him, my anxiety intensified to the point of paralysis. Tears threatened to spill, but he enveloped me in a hug before I could utter a word. I felt safe, at home, and at peace in that embrace. That sense of security was why I stayed with him. He was a constant reminder that I wasn't alone and had someone supporting me. He was consistent. He was safe. He was present. I should be thankful for that. He had driven eighty miles in his mom's Cadillac to see me, and there I was… Ungrateful. I even felt guilty for having lunch with Chad earlier that week. The tears finally descended then. I cried. I cried because my heart was racing so fast that my left arm grew numb. I cried because I felt like shit. I cried because I felt so lost. I felt helpless. I just wanted to be loved. His embrace distracted me from the outside world. I just stood there and smelled him. I listened to his heart until my anxiety decreased just enough for me to speak.

"Can we skip the race?" I asked. He appeared alarmed.

"What's wrong, babe?" he asked, pulling back to look at my face. He saw my red eyes and realized I was panicking.

"Yeah, sure!" he said, rubbing my back and hugging me.

Instead of doing the race, we got Thai food and rested in the room all day in my roommate's absence. I laid on him, and somehow, we both could fit in a twin-sized bed. Man, college was trippy. I was nearly two hundred pounds, and he suffered through the weight of my body without complaint. He kissed me on the forehead, and all was well with the world. I was definitely in love.

"I love you," I said into his chest.

"I love you, too," he said, rubbing my back again. We didn't have sex. He was ok with that. I was ok with that. We talked and held each other all that night. After that day, the way he treated me erased all doubts from my mind. *Chad, who? Michael was my person.*

"Just so you know, you're mine now!" I said, holding him tight around the waist.

"Yes, ma'am!" he said with a melodic base in his voice.

At that point, he was no longer unattractive to me. To me, he was a beautiful human being with a gentle soul. He had trauma from his past, I could tell. Maybe he was bullied. Maybe he was disrespected because of his features… It didn't mean anything to me; I would love him regardless. I had fallen completely in love with him at that point. It was official. We were official. I was determined to cherish that love like it was my lifeline.

I became so engrossed and enamored by the relationship that I even began writing erotica excerpts:

I sat there next to my man in bed, having an honest discussion as he prepared to whip his dick out and give himself a goodnight present. It was his routine. He said that it made him sleep better. Who I am to judge? So, I stare at him for a minute watching him rev himself up preparing for the lift off, but then a conversation from earlier that day came to mind. Now, he isn't easy to cum by any means, so I usually lay beside him and fall asleep while he's doing his business. It was soothing to feel the bed rock in a steady rhythm during 'his' time. Any who, he said, "sometimes I wish you would just go down and do it for me, instead of falling asleep." Now, I have this running through my head as he began to stroke the shaft slowly back and forth, coming up to just below the ridge of the head. I stared down at his hand possessively and knocked his hand out of the way....

Chapter 18

A WALK OF COMPLETION

"The best masterpieces in the world are the direct results of pressure."
~**Sovereign Jane Jenkins**

Jackson, Mississippi
April 27, 2018

Michael was able to get his credits together just in time for graduation, and I couldn't have been more thrilled and proud of him. It was a major relief for both of us because we would be on the same accord for this next stage of life. It was fitting that I moved back to Jackson for him so our relationship could grow and blossom. We could move anywhere and do anything after graduation.

Before heading to graduation, I visited Michael on Friday evening at his friend's house. Her name was Avis. She was quite the firecracker, always speaking her mind without hesitation. Why were most of Michael's friends women? This question lingered in my mind. I observed closely. Did he have a different orientation? Or did he simply relate better to women? He had male friends but hadn't introduced me to them yet. Entering the apartment, I was greeted by bedazzled lamps, plush rugs, and an overall tidy space. Avis was undoubtedly feminine. Michael leaned more towards metrosexual than feminine. I didn't sense any romantic interest from her towards him.

"Hey, babe. This is Avis," Michael introduced me to her.

"Hey, beautiful!" Avis said in a cheery, happy tone. She seemed pleasant enough.

"Hey, Avis! I like your place," I said, looking around. Avis was an attractive woman, but I wasn't insecure enough to believe that she was a better woman than me. I didn't sense that I needed to view her as competition, so I wasn't worried about losing him to her. I was a secure female in general. If he wanted to leave me, go right ahead. I always kept one foot out of the door in double dutch mode. I liked being single and independent. I was still adjusting to relationship life, so I dared him to find someone better.

"Thank you, love! Make yourself at home."

There were six other people around the table at Avis's house. One of them I recognized. It was her boyfriend, John. We had graduated from the same high school. He was two years older than me.

"John! It's good to see you!" I said, pleasantly surprised.

"Hey, what was your name again? I remember your face but not your name," he said.

"No worries. It's Janeka!"

"Oh, yeah. It's nice seeing you again. It's been years."

"Yeah. I look a little different as well. I have lost weight since then," I said merrily.

"Yeah, I could tell. Nice seeing you again," he said, shaking my hand.

"Same!" I said, shaking his hand in return.

"How do y'all know each other?" Michael asked.

"We went to school together," I said matter-of-factly.

"Y'all, we're all graduating tomorrow!" Avis screamed out of nowhere. Everyone was excited and ready for the next stage of life. It was a happiness overload. Everyone in the room was high energy and seemed celebratory in spirit.

"Babe, you didn't get your hair done?" I asked, looking up at Michael. His hair had grown out immensely, and he looked unkempt, even though he didn't smell or anything. However, he needed to look presentable, especially on graduation day.

"Sit down," I said.

"Avis. Do you have any clamps and holding spray so I can secure the front of his hair?" I said, looking over to her.

"Of course," she said, rushing off to her room to search for the necessary things I needed to help Michael look presentable.

"Why didn't you get your hair done?" I asked.

"I didn't have the money," he said, appearing embarrassed. I was mommaing him. His own mother should have made sure that he looked presentable.

"Your mom didn't say anything about your hair?" I asked, annoyed.

"No, she didn't. She's not coming to my graduation," he said sadly.

My eyebrows rose.

WTF! What kind of mother didn't attend her son's graduation? I thought to myself.

"Why?" I asked curiously.

"Because she has to be at the temple," he said in a hushed tone.

"Huh," I said, clearly not hearing him correctly. Was she in a cult? It would take hell and high water to keep me from attending my child's graduation, especially my son's.

I rolled my eyes to the ceiling, realizing that his mom clearly didn't have good sense.

I thought about all the hell my own mom went through with her in-laws.

"She never misses a Saturday. One time, she was so sick that she could barely get out of bed, but she tried to make it to the temple," he said matter-of-factly.

I was genuinely floored then.

"What happened to your mom?" I asked in a hushed tone, away from everyone else in a corner of the room.

"Her mom died, and she felt like it was her fault. She died in the Cadillac on the way to the hospital, and my mom felt guilty for not taking her sooner when she was getting worse, so my mom sort of lost her mind in the process. She found salvation and peace in the temple, so she converted faiths and began to heal in that setting," he said thoughtfully.

Ohh!! It was a trauma response. That makes sense. I wondered why his mom was so standoffish. She's still healing and doesn't like getting close to people.

"She even convinced her sister to do it with her. So, none of them will be there tomorrow," he said, looking like a lost child.

WTF, I thought again. *Still, what kind of mother and family skips their child's graduation? Not a family that I cared to be a part of...*

"I'm sorry, babe," I said, rubbing his back, sensing his silent pain. His gaze was cast downward, avoiding my eyes. He felt devalued. I understood his emotions. I wanted him to know how important he was, especially to me. I bent down slightly and kissed him on the forehead. He looked up at me, a sheepish expression on his face. Avis walked back into the room, holding the items I'd requested.

"Here you go, girl! Have at it!" she said, her excitement evident in her eagerness to help.

I took the clamps and spray, smiling in appreciation.

"Thanks, my love," I said, genuinely grateful. I was determined to help my man look his best. Taking a lock of his hair, I began to twist it, ensuring it would look neat beneath his cap.

***

The next day…

It was Saturday, and I was preparing myself for the grand day ahead. I had bought him a board game, balloons, a card, and a custom-made t-shirt that read, 'Go Mr. Michael Downs!' on the front. I was radiating wifey energy, which was precisely the impression I wanted to make. By then, I was in love, after all. I wanted him to know that I was here to stay and that I'd support him no matter what. I decided to bring my mother at the last minute. His mother wouldn't be attending, but mine would. I hoped it would bring him some comfort, emphasizing how much he meant to me.

"Momma, are you ready?" I asked, hastily gathering all the gifts I'd bought for Michael.

"Yeah, let me use the restroom," she responded, heading towards the back.

I sighed in mild frustration. "Momma, we can't be late! You know the traffic will be a nightmare. We need to leave in five minutes," I called out, ensuring she could hear me through the walls.

"I'm coming!" her voice echoed back. I quickly wrote a message in the graduation card and added twenty dollars as a gift from our family.

"Alright, I'm ready," she announced, entering the room in her vibrant attire. She resembled Mr. Brown from "Meet the Browns" in her fashion choices.

Picnic patterns, neon hues, and black and white stripes were her staples. I appreciated her distinct style; it made it easy to spot her in a crowd. Given her outfits, she was never hard to find. Seeing the silver lining, I always complimented her coordinated looks.

My mother was legally blind, which meant I occasionally had to assist her with certain details regarding her outfits. Sometimes she'd wear her clothes backward, mismatch her eyeshadow, or choose shoes that clashed with her ensemble. As I gave her a final once-over after she appeared from her room, I silently praised God.

'Thank god, she looks decent!' I thought to myself.

"I'm ready!" she said happily.

"Good. Me too!" I said, walking past her with the balloons and gifts.

We made it to the graduation right on time. We watched him and my best friend Shay walk across the stage. She was happy, and so was he. I was happy for them both.

After graduation, I sat waiting for Michael with his gifts in hand. Everyone was so excited for the next stage of life that the energy in the air was magnetic. "Congratulations!" I said once I laid my eyes on him.

He looked up and smiled in surprise because I was holding his gifts.

"Thank you, babe," he said, reaching down to kiss me on the lips, and he gave me a tight hug.

"I love you," he said.

"I love you, too!" I said.

We separated, and I opened my shirt for him to read it.

"Oh, you're trying to get wifed!" he said in excitement while reading the fine print.

"Maybe," I said, blushing.

I stood back from him and then looked around. His father was behind him. His brother had come into town to celebrate, too. I looked around for Gia, but I only saw Vince.

Where's Gia? I thought silently to myself.

Out of his entire family, only five people, including me and my mother, showed up to his graduation.

I felt bad for him because I hoped more of his family would have come, but it was *Saturday*.

Pussy Policy #54: Don't let your empathy turn you into someone's victim.

I rolled my eyes in frustration. Poor Michael. I know he felt less than a human being then, but I didn't let him feel sorry for himself for one second.

"Momma, this is Michael's brother, Nathan," I said, gesturing Nathan's way.

"It's nice to meet you," my mother said, shaking Nathan's hand.

"Nice to meet you," Nathan said, shaking my mom's hand.

Nathan was bigger than his brother muscle-wise. I could tell he spent much time in the gym working on his upper body. I could tell protein was his best friend, too. Nathan was more attractive than Michael physically, but they had similar features. I didn't really see Nathan in a sexual light, though, out of respect for Michael. I found their relationship odd, though. They never hugged like brothers. In my family, hugging was customary and downright expected. His family seemed anti-affection. It confused me because I was naturally a hugger and loved people. Well, certain people. Why weren't they loving each other?

It's not our nature, I remember Michael saying.

Vince walked up to Michael and shook his hand, "Congratulations, man!"

"Thank you!" Michael said, shaking Vince's hand and doing the side man-hug thing.

Hmmmm. Interesting, I thought to myself. We said our goodbyes and separated. We planned to have dinner with Michael's dad, Mr. Tommy, Nathan, and Nathan's girlfriend, Maya. But Michael needed to go home and change first. He was sweaty under the armpits due to the Mississippi heat and was wearing a formal shirt, tie, and pants that did not necessarily fit his frame correctly. I made a mental note to go shopping with him once he got a stable and secure job. I couldn't wait until that day came. Hopefully, he wouldn't be so cheap.

"Let's go see *Endgame*!" His family agreed in unison, while I was opposed to it. I only watched new Marvel movies with my brothers. It was tradition, and if our relationship didn't work out, I didn't want the memories of watching a Marvel movie with him, especially not the premier. I wanted it with my brother.

"What?" I said, hesitating. "I only watch those movies with my brother," I said, wanting to back out and let him, his brother, and his father go watch it.

"Babe, it's my graduation! I want you there," he said matter-of-factly.

I sighed heavily, "Ok."

This may sound weird, but I didn't want him tainting these movies for me if our relationship was unsuccessful.

***

Hattiesburg, Mississippi
May 11, 2018

It was my big day—the most significant day of my life: Graduation Day! Finally freed from the confines of nursing school, my excitement was palpable. I nearly performed a silent fist pump as I prepared. Slipping into my sparkly dress, I combed through my long, bone-straight tresses and applied my makeup. I felt and looked like a million bucks. Michael had stayed with me the previous night, planning to help me move out after the graduation. Donning my bedazzled cap and plain black gown, I embarked on the trek across campus to the coliseum.

Though I'd sent Gia an invitation, I received no word from her. Perhaps it didn't matter in the grand scheme of things; we all had our own paths to tread.

Entering the coliseum with Michael, I posed for photos with my scholarship mentors. As a Luckyday Scholar, their support ensured I was graduating with minimal debt. The pride was evident in Michael's eyes as he captured the moments. The surreal realization hit me: a new chapter awaited. Unsure of the upcoming adventures, my optimism for the future remained undeterred. Handing my bag to Michael, I proceeded to my designated seat, surrounded by a sea of joyous graduates.

When my moment came, I rose gracefully. Approaching the stage, I internally prayed against any missteps that might steal the spotlight. As the announcer inquired about the pronunciation of my name, pride swelled within me. "It's Ja-Neek-a," I responded, relishing the melodic cadence of my own name.

His smooth voice resonated, "Next graduate is Janeka J..., *Magna Cum Laude*..." I glided across the stage, the thunderous applause of my family filling the air. Their enthusiastic support was a poignant reminder: I wasn't alone on this journey. As I progressed, a foundational memory sparked within me:

As I passed my father in the hallway on my way to the living room, I felt an unease. I was seldom nearby when both my parents occupied the same space. He would often shoo me away or silence me, telling me to "be quiet." But I'd speak up, regardless. No one could silence me, not even him. It didn't matter if he was my newfound biological father; I stood up for my freedom of speech. I might have failed the first grade, but that didn't mean I was unintelligent. I had a voice, and what I said mattered. Even when he'd brusquely tell me to "be quiet," I refused to be permanently silenced. As I settled on the floor to play with my new Bratz Doll, my thoughts were disrupted by an odor emanating from the bathroom where Chayne was. Not wanting to venture towards my room, I continued playing until a loud commotion from my mother's room jolted me. The yells and screams signaled it wasn't some natural occurrence, but my father's rage.

I sprang up and rushed toward the sound, but Chayne, coming out of the bathroom, overtook me. As I reached the scene, I was met with a terrifying sight: my father held my mother by the neck, her body wrapped in a shower curtain, suspended over the bathtub. The hair rollers she'd recently put in were strewn across the tub, evidence of the violence of his actions.

Horrified, tears streamed down my face. "Don't hurt her!" I pleaded.

Chayne managed to wrestle our father away, pinning him onto the bed. Seizing the opportunity, my mother sprang into action, pummeling him with blows. From my vantage point, the sight was surreal, almost reminiscent of a toy fight—until he cried out for a pause as though it was a mere game.

"Mama, stop!" I intervened.

"Move! He's hurting Chayne!" she responded, her focus unwavering.

In a desperate bid, Tony managed to free his face from the bed cover, sinking his teeth deep into her forearm. Her anguished scream prompted me to act. I struck him with all my strength, causing him to release his grip. Once freed, my mother rushed to tend to her bleeding arm, which bore the grim mark of his bite.

The trauma of that night etched itself deeply into my memory. The next day in social studies, I paid rapt attention under Mr. Smallwood's guidance. Determined to make a difference, I excelled academically, believing that someday, my knowledge might offer an escape for my mother if she couldn't find her own way out. The lure of the money in Tony's safe wasn't worth enduring his abuse. With resolve, I powered through high school and graduated with an impressive 4.3 GPA.

"Go, Janeka!" I heard Michael shout as I completed my walk across the stage, marking the end of my college journey. Although Tony, my father, wasn't present, I didn't shed tears. Instead, I reveled in my accomplishments, held my head high, and exited the stage, finally proud of the transformation that began in the 7th grade. Strangely enough, if Tony hadn't knocked out my mother's rollers that day, I might not have been on that stage. So, in an unusual way, something positive emerged from that traumatic experience. I had become someone who valued free education, a rarity. Typically, people often undervalue what comes free or easily, taking it for granted. I scanned the crowd, spotting my family, and smiled. It truly was a splendid day, tinged with some bitterness but overwhelmingly sweet.

Almost my entire family attended my graduation. Absent were my eldest brother, my ex-stepfather, my biological father, and a few cousins. The absence of my biological father stung; after all, part of my journey was because of him. Perhaps I wasn't significant in his eyes. But, glancing at the smiling faces of my family, my spirits soared. They were here. In contrast, Michael's family had been absent from his own graduation. While I felt sympathy for him, I couldn't let it overshadow my joy. He was with me, and I hoped he was enjoying the day too. The numerous sashes draped around my neck, complemented by medals, were becoming cumbersome. Handing them to my jubilant mother, I couldn't help but grin. She wore custom t-shirts with my face printed on them, distributed to everyone present. It gave the impression of a memorial rather than a celebration, but she was undeterred. She wanted everyone to know about her daughter's achievement, regardless of any judgements. This unapologetic enthusiasm and thoughtfulness was what endeared her to me; I had inherited her can-do spirit.

"I love you, momma!" I said, embracing her.

"I love you more!" she replied, tightening the hug.

The countless hours of late-night studying, sleep deprivation, tears, stress, and anxiety all felt worthwhile in that moment. Yet, I was uncertain if I'd ever willingly endure such a journey again. Afterward, we all dined together, celebrating not just my graduation but also my cousin's birthday. Smiling, I reached for Michael's hand.

"I love you!" I said to him,

"I love you, too!" he said, tapping me on the nose with the pad of his finger.

I smiled, and he smiled back at me. The future seemed so bright for us both.

I looked around and acknowledged all of my family's presence. I was truly appreciative of their being there. I was beyond blessed to have all of them around.

***

We all decided to grab dinner at a seafood restaurant. Michael sat to my left; Auntie Ruby, Auntie Sarah Lee, Mama, Mason, Chayne, and his wife Tina sat around the table. We were busy ordering food while Auntie Ruby was rumbling on and on.

"Chayne, why didn't you finish college?" Auntie Ruby asked suddenly.

Why the hell would she ask that at my graduation?

I looked towards Mama; she looked like she could have stabbed Auntie Ruby in the hand with her fork. I could see the vein popping out of said hand from across the table.

"Because it wasn't what I wanted…" Chayne said, trailing off, visibly agitated by the line of questioning also.

Awkward was an understatement; I felt downright uncomfortable.

"Well, I was just thinking about you never graduating because if I had the funds, I would have paid for you to finish…" Auntie Ruby said, stirring the pot and implying that he was a charity case.

Oh, Lord! Please don't let them fight today. I didn't need any trauma on my special day.

"Why would you go there?" Mama finally spoke up and stepped in.

Michael also appeared to be uncomfortable at my side because he was quiet for a change; he was typically a talker, which worked perfectly for our relationship. I was introverted, but that was no help at the moment.

"Do you guys need anything else?"

Saved by the waiter.

"Yes, could I have a glass of champagne for this joyous occasion?" I said loudly, casting a glance in Mama's direction, silently pleading with my eyes for her to drop the topic, even though I knew she couldn't see me clearly. However, she could discern from my tone that the conversation needed to be postponed.

"So, when are y'all going to have babies?" Auntie Lyn asked Chayne and his wife.

"When the good Lord sees fit," Chayne responded with a deadpan tone. It was evident he was growing weary of that question from her, but he managed to keep a stoic expression.

"Are y'all trying?" Michael inquired.

"Man, I've been 'shooting up the club' for a year now and still no luck."

"Ick!" I exclaimed, feigning covering my ears. "TMI!" I added, visibly bothered.

"Oh, hush!" Chayne retorted, laughing.

Michael joined in the laughter, but I was too taken aback to even muster a smile.

None of that was my business, so I focused on finishing up my seafood pot pie.

I still hadn't heard anything from Gia. Princess Gia probably just wanted to continue to be the center of attention. Fine by me. I'll starve her. "Back to the regularly scheduled program," I thought to myself while looking around the table.

Chapter 19

SHE LOVES ME, SHE LOVES ME NOT

Drop the act,
Listen to the drumming of my heart.
Feel me, skin-to-skin
While remembering the start.
Although the frostbite is pulsing along our veins
I fear the day when life will tear us apart.
~Sovereign Jane Jenkins

Jackson, Mississippi
June 4, 2018

Pussy Policy #55: Never stay in a relationship just to get close and stay close to someone else.

"Gia needs help tonight selling a chair," Michael said while playing his game. "I have to work, but I volunteered you," he added, glancing my way. I tried to ignore the fact that he'd been on the PlayStation for the past four hours. Did he have any personal goals that would inspire him to step away from the game and get out of the house? He spent so much time with friends or next to me that I began to wonder if he truly knew who he was as a man. It seemed like he couldn't bear silence when alone. That's when I did my best thinking. How could one think independently when constantly surrounded by others? I prayed that if we ever married, I wouldn't find myself raising a little boy in a man's body. Playing a game every single day wouldn't cut it for me. I needed someone productive and creative, not just a reservoir of wasted potential lounging on a couch or bed. Playing for a couple of hours a week? Understandable. But spending countless hours of one's life in a single spot was untenable. I sighed, pondering solutions to what I perceived as his issues, inadvertently making his challenges my own. No steady job, no reliable car, no apartment, no enlightening books. He could potentially hinder my progress in life, or I could accelerate his. I genuinely hoped we could make it work. Was this the rollercoaster nature of relationships? He already had my virginity. The idea of starting over with someone else was daunting.

"Ok...." My response was delayed, my thoughts having strayed elsewhere. Right! Gia's chair. Why would she need assistance with that? It seemed straightforward.

"She's selling it to a stranger through an online platform, and Vince will be at work," he elaborated.

"That does sound risky, especially here in Jackson, Mississippi. I'm on it," I said, settling next to him on the bed.

"Great, I'll let Gia know," he replied, swiftly texting on his phone.

I found it odd that she needed help with a chair so soon after our recent visit. Perhaps my imagination was overactive. Maybe it was simple wishful thinking or nothing serious. Or, was it a ploy to pick up where we left off the previous week? Whatever the reason, I'd find out later that day.

***

Later That Evening…

As I drove to Gia's place alone, my stomach churned with nerves from the previous night at work. I had witnessed the death of my first patient as a student nurse, and I desperately wanted someone to discuss it with. The way he just slipped away before my eyes, the pale coolness in his gaze, and the despair on his family's faces were profoundly affecting my mental well-being. While I was a nurse by profession, I also deeply valued human life as an empath. Every emotion resonated with me on a spiritual level. Perhaps that's why I was so selective about who could touch me. For the sake of my mental health and personal self-preservation, I allowed very few—among patients, family, and friends—to come into physical contact with me.

I arrived at Gia's in less than 20 minutes. Throughout the night, my thoughts dwelled on my recent experience at the hospital. The grief of families always hit me hard. It consumed me. I could never easily forget the pain they went through, always carrying a piece of their sorrow in my heart. I approached Gia and Vince's apartment, making sure to be aware of my surroundings, especially since I was in Jackson, Mississippi. After a second or two, Gia opened the door. Dressed in a thick sweater, pants, and UGG boots, she looked cozy—typical for her since she was always cold. I reminded myself that she was expecting other company as well, not just me.

"Hey, girl!" I said, walking over the threshold.

"Hey!" she curtly said, leaving me at the door and walking off with not so much as a hug or real greeting. I blinked in an unsurprised way. It seemed she was walled off.

"How was your day?" I continued, just making conversation.

"It was good!" she said while looking down at her phone, not looking me in the eye or towards my way.

"Hmmm," I said before I could stop myself. I guess my day or week didn't matter to her. It seemed to be Gia's world once again. I rolled my eyes again, unable to stop the assault of thoughts on my psyche. She had a surefire way about her that pissed people off, but she often got away with it since she was an 'attractive' woman.

"My day was good as well. It was slightly dreary because I had witnessed my first death in my profession as a new nurse. So, I'm just trying to understand the death process," I said honestly.

"Oh, the lady is almost here," she said, walking towards the door and looking down at her phone.

I looked down at the chairs in question. They were baby blue and quirky-looking. I could see why she was selling them. They didn't go with the theme in the living room.

"Vince and I are moving, so we're getting rid of stuff," she said, looking out the door. *Baby, whether y'all moving or not, these need to be sold,* I thought to myself.

She also had her purse next to the door. She was packing her nine-millimeter, aka her gun. I was looking like, 'Woah, she's for real'. I heard someone outside coming, so it was showtime. I stood up, ready to assist with the chairs.

"I guess we can't be too careful, now can we?" I said, walking over to one of the chairs and preparing to pick one of them up.

"Hey, How are you doing?" I heard a lady outside ask Gia.

"Great! How are you?" Gia said in her chipper tone.

Gia stepped back from the door and allowed the lady and a man who appeared to be her husband to walk into the apartment.

"I'm Gia, and that's my friend Janeka," she gestured my way.

"Hey, how are you?" I asked politely.

"Good. I'm Missy, and this is my husband, Leroy."

"Hey, Missy and Leroy!" I said, trying not to be awkward.

"So, these are the chairs?" Missy asked, walking over to the obnoxious blue pieces of furniture inspecting them like they were a work of art.

"I love them!" she exclaimed.

My eyes bulged as I looked at the chairs once again.

What the heck was she looking at? I thought to myself.

"Awesome! It took a while for me to get these painted, but I loved the end result. We're getting rid of them because we're moving! " Gia happily said, clapping her hands together.

I kept my mouth shut because that gasp would have been audible.

"I'm so happy I looked in the marketplace for them! How much are all of them?"

"Seventy-five dollars," Gia said, expectantly looking into her face to gauge her reaction.

"Ok!" Missy said, turning to her husband, that had the same look on his face that I had on mine. He scratched his head silently. He looked like the epitome of the saying: 'Happy wife, Happy life.'

I smiled inwardly as his wife quickly handed Gia the seventy-five dollars.

"What are you going to do with the furniture?" Gia asked out of curiosity as the husband was about to grab the first chair.

"We're opening a café in our community. We are so excited for this new venture." Missy smiled at her husband, and he looked at peace with her decisions. That's the kind of man that I needed in my life.

"We wanted different pieces that would complement the shop's ambience, and this would be perfect for it," Missy said.

Gia looked honored to have had the opportunity to provide the chairs. She even grabbed her chest dramatically. 'Oh, brother,' I thought to myself.

They chatted a minute or two further.

"Alright, dear, we left the kids in the car," the husband said in a reassuring yet reminding tone.

Each of us picked up a chair and headed to the door and downstairs with the pieces. We dropped them next to the truck; the couple came in and said our goodbyes.

Gia and I returned to the apartment. I had left my purse, and I had to pee.

"Well, easy enough," I said, walking towards the bathroom.

"Yep," Gia said, folding her money into her purse.

I came out of the bathroom, and Gia was in the kitchen on the phone with Vince. I silently said my goodbyes as she went on and on about the chairs with Vince over the phone. She waved at me, indicating it was time for me to exit. I waved silently as I walked out of the door. I laughed to myself, not at all surprised at the sheer selfishness. I didn't expect much from her outside of a 'thank you,' but a piece of me was disappointed in the way she brushed me off. I thought about it as I rode back across town.

"What exactly were Gia's real motives? Did she not want me and Michael together? Did she like me for herself? What was her real deal?" I couldn't figure her out completely, and it messed with me. Would I have liked for something else to happen? On a superficial level, yes, simply because my ego was hurt. I sighed in annoyance and thought about my patient who had died. I wondered if he suffered before my shift began. A tear almost came to my eye as I thought about how precious life truly was.

My phone began to ring as I turned onto the highway. It was Michael. Good, I needed that distraction.

"Hey, babe," I said on the first ring.

"Hey, Neka! How did it go?"

"It went well. The couple was from south Mississippi and loved the chairs," I said.

"And…" he said and paused.

"And, nothin. That was it. Now, I'm headed back home."

"Did you stay after they left?" he asked unabashedly.

"No, she called Vince, and then I left. That's all there is to it," I said sternly.

"Ok," he said in a disappointed voice.

"What's up?" I was curious about his line of questioning.

"Oh, nothing," he said.

"Did you set me up?" I said, not believing that he would be so devious.

"I don't know what you're talking about, " he said, laughing.

"You wanted something to happen, didn't you?" I asked in disbelief.

"It wouldn't bother me," he said nonchalantly.

"Why?" I said curiously.

"Janeka, you have a whole bear named after her. Are you really going to try to tell me that there's nothing there?"

I sighed because he was right in a way.

"Nothing happened, Michael," I said, focusing on the road, "it's not like that at all."

"Ok…"

"And please don't volunteer me for anything else Gia-related. She has five siblings. She can adopt one of them for an evening," I said seriously.

"Ok," he said snickering.

I didn't find anything amusing, but who knew what tickled his funny bone? After hanging up with him, I reflected on the kiss with Gia again. She was evidently bi-curious, yet she had chosen a 'holier-than-thou' attire for the evening, clearly signaling her disinterest. I respected that. I understood boundaries. Smirking, I looked back on the game night. It was just a good time—nothing more, nothing less. Although I initially entered a relationship to grow closer to Gia, over time, my feelings deepened for Michael and dwindled for Gia. She was turning into a constant annoyance. Perhaps I wasn't really into women after all. Interestingly, I hadn't found men attractive until my experience with Michael, and I often wondered if it was linked to unresolved feelings about my father.

Chapter 20

A LOVE LOST

*"Love is beautiful,
Love is sweet,
The only love that I want in the world
is a love that I can keep."*
-Sovereign Jane Jenkins

It was our seven-month anniversary, and I felt Michael couldn't comprehend the pain of rejection from two fathers. He only knew the sting of being rejected by a woman, most recently by his ex. Such pain was indescribable, and I had no desire to articulate it to him. Regardless of how much I tried to explain, he would never grasp it. The man I had believed was my father had so callously evicted his own biological son, Darren, from the house as a teenager. Given that, I shouldn't have been shocked by his rejection of me upon learning I wasn't his biological daughter. To him, Chayne and I seemed expendable, merely two fewer bills to fret about.

"Are you going to talk to me?" he inquired, sitting on my bed. It had been two days since my last visit to the old house I grew up in. I was weary of his inexplicable absence from my life. He didn't love me. He had relayed to Darren that my visit to his home was just a ploy to stir up drama. I remained in disbelief. Having been avoiding my mother altogether, I was mortified that I'd even entertained the idea of opening that door to clear the air. Clearly, reconciliation wasn't feasible, nor was it healthy for me.

"Is everything ok now?" Michael asked.

"Yes… It'll be just fine," I said confidently as he grabbed my hand and kissed the top of it.

"I brought you your favorite drink," he said, holding up the cold iced tea. I smirked.

"Thank you, babe!" I said, kissing him, genuinely impressed with his thoughtful gesture.

"It's about time," I said.

"Oh, hush!" he said, laughing.

"What! Gifts are my love language," I said honestly.

"You want every day to be Christmas, so I'm not surprised."

"Umm, it better be! I know my worth!" I said, getting up.

"Alright, get dressed! Let's go out on the town," he said.

"Yay!" I said, squealing as I jumped up from the bed and got dressed.

Contrary to my overall mood, I looked good, but sometimes you gotta fake it until you make it.

"You look good," Michael said, kissing me on the forehead.

"Thank you so much! Let's go!" I said, running towards the door.

***

We ended up going to the mall for ice cream and later visited a speakeasy located at the back of a diner in Jackson. It was an unexpected venue, but I chose to keep an open mind. They offered unique drinks with a high alcohol content. Though it wasn't to my taste, I feigned appreciation because I didn't want to give Michael the wrong impression. I was grateful for the gesture, but I questioned whether he truly grasped my needs on a spiritual and emotional level. I sighed, trying to enjoy the moment, but, disappointingly, my favorite part of the evening was leaving the speakeasy. I wasn't looking to drown my sorrows in alcohol. A movie and dinner would have suited me better. I longed for an escape from reality, weary from the constant blows life had been dealing me. I yearned to lose myself in the narrative of someone else's imagination.

We got into the car and prepared to head home.

Michael turned to me, "How do you feel now?"

"Crappy," I said honestly.

He appeared sad because he realized he had failed to cheer me up. I didn't want to give him the satisfaction of thinking he could heal me. I depended on my family only for that. So, if he ever cheated on me or hurt me, I had the satisfaction of knowing that I would be just fine without him. It might have been the trauma talking.

"I'm sick of trying to please my father... One rejected me, one made me feel bad for needing money for school, and the other I purposely pushed away because I didn't think he'd ever understand me. It wasn't because he was white, but it was because I was tired of loving a father just to lose him later on. I wanted stability."

"You need money for school?" he asked.

"Needed. He let me borrow three thousand dollars for a college class. He expects me to pay it back after graduation, " I said.

"I'll pay for it," Michael said.

I smiled, "You can't do that without a real job, and I don't want you doing that without a real job," I said, smiling at the offer.

"I'm just saying that's fucked up. I want to be with you and ensure you're taken care of. I want to marry you!" he said. I felt warm in my stomach at the statement. All I ever wanted in this world was the love of a man that would stand the test of time.

"Thank you…" I said as I kissed him from the driver's seat.

Time would tell how sincere he was. We will see where this goes together.

Pussy Policy #56: A man will promise you the moon, the stars, and the sky; make sure those promises have merit by watching actions.

Although everything with Michael was sounding good, I needed to see action. Although he didn't have a reliable car or a real job and still lived with his parents, I believed in him. I believed in us. We could make it. What's meant will be. One thing I knew for certain was that I had to pay Tony back, whether I was with Michael or not.

***

"Mama, we saw Aunt Karrie out at the mall. She was cleaning up the bathrooms there," I said as I and Michael walked into the house.

Mama paused as she held the spoon of ice cream up to her mouth, and a look of agitation came across her countenance. It was fleeting but observable.

"Oh, really? Did she speak?"

"Yes, ma'am. I barely recognized her. She had picked up some weight but was still a beautiful woman."

Mama's face said, "fuck that bitch," but her mouth said, "Good for her," as she returned to eating her ice cream.

I glanced at Michael, and he shrugged.

"That was weird," he said as we entered my room.

"Yeah, it's a long story," I said.

"I could tell. Spare me the details."

"My pleasure," I said, sitting on my bed.

Mama and I still hadn't spoken much since the incident; she was horrible with words, and I was horrible with my emotions. It seemed to be safer that way.

***

As Michael and I sat in the pews of the funeral home, lost in our grief, the man I had believed was my biological father entered, casting a palpable tension throughout the room.

Daddy? Why was he here? Who had invited him?

The more heart-wrenching moment was when he, the man who had raised me since birth, walked right past me upon seeing me, as if I were a mere phantom.

"Unbelievable," I whispered, my defenses instantly rising. If he could behave so coldly, then trust in anyone seemed uncertain. From that moment, I began questioning everyone's loyalty. It became a case of being guilty until proven innocent. It was a traumatic response, and I was at a loss for how to address the emotions.

Later that evening, tears flowed freely as I nestled into Michael's embrace, my mind toggling between past and present. He was familiar with my insecurities and continually assured me of his steadfast presence, regardless of who might abandon me. As much as I aimed to maintain a strong façade in front of Michael, every woman has her limit. My resolve had shattered in regards to Daddy. It was clear I would never attempt reconciliation with him again. My thoughts drifted to the last time I saw Daddy's mother, Grandma.

I pondered on her possible reaction had she witnessed his actions that day. Even though she wasn't my biological grandmother, our bond was genuine, and she cherished me as her own until her final moment.

I looked over my shoulder as I snuck through the gate of the nursing home. I had obtained the code from my former cousin while out at a store. I knew I wasn't supposed to be there, but I needed to see the woman who had helped raise me, even if it was for the last time. I hadn't seen Daddy in years, and it had been even longer since I'd seen her. She was aging, and her health was declining. I had heard from my oldest brother that she was bedridden and weakening daily. Her time on Earth was nearing its end, so I was determined to say goodbye before it was too late.

Walking down the hallway, I recognized her last name on a door. As I entered the room, the familiar scent of hair grease and cocoa butter filled my nostrils, reminding me of bygone days. Grandma was engrossed in her TV shows. Eight years had passed since our last goodbye. Her lustrous silver hair was plaited on the sides. With her Native American Indian features, mixed with Black heritage, and her long silver hair, she looked radiant. Having known her as a short, round woman for most of my life, it was no surprise to see her bedridden. Gout, a result of her lifestyle choices, had taken a toll.

Setting aside the strain between Daddy and me, I smiled, hoping she'd remember me. "Hey, Grandma!" I greeted her hesitantly.

She glanced my way, initially appearing bewildered. But then, recognition dawned, and she beamed, showing off a gummy grin. "Tootie! My Tootie!" she exclaimed.

I approached, embracing her gently. Her arms, heavy and frail, tried to hug back. Overwhelmed with emotion, I murmured, "Grandma..."

"Tootie... How have you been?" she asked as we parted.

"I've been good," I replied, absorbing the precious moment. We conversed for hours. I undid her hair, brushing it just as I did when I was younger.

"Grandma, I miss your biscuits. I'd love one with some Blackburn syrup," I remarked wistfully.

"I'll make you some when I'm better," she replied with a melancholy smile.

We shared that moment of hope, even if reality suggested otherwise. When a nurse, Sarah, arrived with Grandma's lunch, Grandma introduced me proudly. "This is my granddaughter. She's going to be a nurse one day."

Sarah, smiling, set down the tray and offered, "Would you like to feed her?"

"Of course," I agreed, feeding Grandma, reminded of when our roles were reversed.

Grandma's unwavering love, despite discovering I wasn't her biological granddaughter, was evident. I wished her son had shown the same strength. As evening approached, I needed to head home to avoid raising suspicions—I was still in high school.

"I'll see you later, Grandma," I said, planting a kiss on her cheek.

"Alright, Tootie. I love you, hear!"

"I love you too. Always have. Always will," I affirmed.

As I exited, I stole one last glance. She watched me from behind her bed railing, and I smiled, leaving her in solitude.

That was the last time that I saw her alive.

Grandma passed away three months later. I thanked God for allowing me to say my final goodbye.

Chapter 21

THE ACCIDENT

*"Life is teemed with pain.
No one ever really feels quite the same.
You become a completely different person
that adapts to the change."*
~Sovereign Jane Jenkins

Jackson, Mississippi
July 10, 2018

In my first week of orientation as an RN, I already found myself questioning my decision to become a nurse. Nothing was straightforward; there seemed to be a thousand ways to do a single task. By the second day, I was rolling my eyes. The sessions felt tedious yet informative. Everything dragged on. I was tempted to text everyone on my phone out of sheer boredom, but I didn't want to risk getting in trouble, so I left my phone in my bag. At one point, I felt my watch vibrate—a sign that I'd received a call. Glancing down, I noticed it was Michael. I had to press 'ignore' and decided I'd call him back later.

Up front, the presenter droned on, and it took all my effort to stay awake. "The culture of our organization is care–" she began, and I was on the verge of dozing off when she announced a break.

Thank the Lord above, I thought. This is really testing my patience.

Stepping out into the hallway, I attempted to return Michael's call, but it went straight to voicemail. That was unusual; he was typically out and about at this hour. After all, it wasn't as if he had a regular job. Shrugging it off, I headed back into the auditorium for another grueling two and a half hours. Michael still hadn't returned my call by the time we wrapped up. Exhausted, the last thing on my mind was visiting him. I was mentally drained and longed for the comfort of my bed.

Michael's friend Mark had sent me a message through social media. That was weird because I didn't believe in following the friends of the men that I dated. I read the message anyway.

Messenger:

Mark: Michael was in a car accident.
Say, What! I screamed as I walked out of the hospital.

I jumped in my car and headed straight for Michael's mother's house. I knew it was probably bad, but I hoped it wasn't life-threatening. I pulled up to the house. There was no sign of Michael's car in sight. I knew that it was probably bad. I swallowed as I walked to the door. His father answered the door as I was about to knock on the front door. I guess he was expecting me.

"Hey!" he said, "He's in his room." He pointed towards Michael's room. I walked down the hallway leading to Michael's room. The door was closed. That was weird. His door was usually always open. I opened the door slowly and saw him lying in bed and his mother sitting in a chair beside the bed.

I could tell they were in a deep conversation.

I walked further into the room, and they both finally looked up.

I saw the cast covering Michael's right foot and knew it was most likely shattered.

How badly was the question….

They both looked gloomy. At least he wasn't dead. No major organs were broken. I hoped.

He looked battered and bruised, sad and in pain. I saw the painkillers on the dresser.

"Hey, Janeka," his mother said grimly.

"Hey…" I said sadly.

She stood up and left the room.

I sat in her place and stared down at Michael. He looked like he had gotten hit by the car.

"Hey," he said.

"So, it's broken?"

"Yes… Shattered…" he said while grimacing.

"What else is wrong?" Something else was in the air but not being said.

"I called Rene to the car accident scene when you didn't pick up the phone," he said quietly.

My stress level began to peak, and I felt my face getting hot.

"Why would you do that?" I asked, genuinely hurt.

"Because you didn't answer the phone," he said.

Oh, he was too bold for that shit. Who does that?

"Oh, ok then…" I said. I was checking out mentally. I was already tired and had no desire to argue with him, especially after my day.

"Well, what is broken?"

Outside of trust….

"My foot is completely broken and has to be reset tomorrow. My right shoulder was dislocated, and I have some generalized soreness," he said, taken aback by my calm response.

I suppose he was expecting an outburst, but I didn't react that way.

To be honest, I was just relieved that he was okay. I had a headache and felt guilty about not answering the phone in the first place. I could have stepped out into the hallway to take his call, but I didn't.

I should have answered the phone.

I quieted my anxieties once I saw him. I was so panicked on my ride over here that I just dismissed the fact that he called his ex to the accident scene. I wanted him truly to just focus on healing. It was my empathy that had me feeling this way.

I had every right to be pissed, didn't I?

I needed to conserve the rest of my mental energy, and he needed to conserve his energy for healing. It was all a process. I could leave Michael today, yes. We had only been together for six months. It wouldn't hurt as bad because of the lack of time invested.

But that would mean I wasted the last six months of my life. I hated wasting time…

I really did love Michael. I had hoped he would change, but the truth was right before me. He was never going to change unless I walked away forever. Yet, forever seemed so long.

Pussy Policy #57: Never try to change a man, but require that he change; don't hesitate to let him go if he refuses.

Notice I didn't take the advice of others with more experience than me in the dating realm and see how this story ends because of it.

Chapter 22

THE SETTLEMENT

Money and love do not coincide.
But generosity and devotion can stand the restraints of time.
Give me love over money always, of course.
But true love is a giver, whether rich or poor.
~Sovereign Jane Jenkins

Jackson, Mississippi
August 21, 2018

It took months for Michael to completely recover from his injuries. Thankfully, my mother had found him a good lawyer to handle his case. While he was unsure about the compensation he would receive, the only thing that truly mattered was his health. Forget the car... Forget the money... I just wanted him to heal and get better. He could always earn money again, but his life was irreplaceable. After a few days of visiting him post-work and post-operation, I noticed a distinct odor emanating from Michael.

"When was the last time you took a shower?" I asked, making a face of disgust.

Michael looked embarrassed. It was evident he hadn't showered in days, and all the while, his mother was in the living room, engrossed in a phone call about the accident instead of attending to her son. Clearly, the poor guy needed some help.

"Huh?" he said.

"You heard me…"

"It's been a couple of days…"

Oh Hell naw!

"Get up!!" I said while pulling him up, carefully not to bump his sore leg but balancing him on his good leg.

"This is totally wifey shit, but we gotta get you clean…" I said, grabbing his crutches and handing them to him, imploring him to follow me into the bathroom.

I went into the bathroom and ran some tepid water. I threw in some Epsom salt for soreness, wrapped his cast with a garbage bag gently and helped him into the tub. I washed him from head to toe. I even removed a layer of his cast to shave the dead skin off of his foot. The dust was permeating the air, and I nearly gagged.

If I didn't get a ring after all of this, I knew something…

"There! All better!" I said, wrapping his hair into a man bun at the top of his head with a towel while he sat on the bed looking perplexed. He hated being helpless, but I was there to help. I was a nurse, after all.

"Thank you, babe!" he said.

I kissed him deeply and slowly. His leg might've been broken, but his penis was not. He was aroused. He was such a man.

"Now is not the time…" I said to him.

"Tell him that…" he smirked.

"Ok…" I dropped to my knees and pulled his penis out of his gym pants to relay the message. It took a couple of minutes for us to get on one accord, but after a few hard lessons, his penis got the point and exploded. Michael was holding on to his bed for dear life while trying not to make a sound because his door was cracked open per his parents' rules.

"Feel better?" I said, standing back up..

"I'm going to fuck you up," he said with clenched teeth.

"Not the response I was hoping for, but whatever, dude!" I said, grabbing my bag and turning towards the door. It was late, and I had to work in the morning.

"Janeka…" he said while catching my hand, "Thank you…." he said while kissing the back of it.

"Don't mention it…" I winked as I walked out of his room.

* * *

Jackson, Mississippi
November 1, 2018

The more time that passed, the more Michael regained his strength. I looked up from my laptop and noticed that he was up and walking around with a slight limp.

"Where's your boot?" I asked incredulously.

He was supposed to remain in the boot for four months. It was only the beginning of month three, and here he was being hard-headed.

"It's in the closet," he said, entering the room. I rolled my eyes. The nurse in me was screaming 'bloody murder' in my head.

He's going to break it again, Lord… He never listens to me.

"Why isn't it on your foot?" I asked with more authority in my voice.

"It's fine…" he said while shrugging off my opinion.

We went to Walmart later that day, and you can bet I made Michael keep the brace on as he rode around on the electric scooter with a basket while I shopped for groceries. His mood was sullen; his head hung low and his hands remained in his pockets when he wasn't operating the scooter. His once buoyant pride now seemed diminished due to his current state of vulnerability. There was a vacant look in his eyes. I could tell he was slipping into a deep depression. However, I tried to buoy his spirits, reminding him that he had me by his side.

"Hey, Big Papa!" I joked, wrapping my arms around him and planting a kiss on his cheek.

"Hey! Why do you have to be such a weirdo?" he laughed.

"Because you love this weirdo," I responded, giving his cheek another peck.

This time, he turned so our lips met.

"Alrighty, let's finish up and head home," he said, his spirits lifting slightly.

"Yes, sir! I'm almost done. Just a few more items," I replied, heading towards the chip aisle.

As I was stretching to grab a bag from the top shelf, someone called out, "Hey, Janeka!"

I glanced over and recognized my neighbors and their spouse. "Hey, guys!" I greeted, waving.

My gaze shifted to Michael, whom they hadn't officially met. "This is my boyfriend, Michael," I introduced.

At the mention of his name, he seemed to shrink a bit, almost like he felt diminished in his current state. I gave him a sympathetic smile. As an empath, I often absorbed others' emotions, feeling what they felt. In that moment, my heart went out to him, and I loved him even more, knowing he needed that support.

"It was nice seeing you guys!" I said to my neighbors, swiftly grabbing some chips from a reachable shelf. I walked back to Michael, dropping them into his basket, keen to leave. He didn't want to be perceived as helpless, and I understood that. During this time, Gia hadn't visited him at all while he was bedridden. Some 'best friend' she turned out to be. His brother also didn't make the effort to see him. However, I was by his side day in and day out, monitoring his recovery, ensuring his mental well-being remained stable. Clearly, his so-called 'friend' and his family weren't as invested. Mark, however, did visit a few times and kept him company. Out of all Michael's friends, Mark seemed genuinely relieved to see him still alive and well.

But for some reason, he and Michael had the most beef.

"He talked to my ex after our first break-up, so I don't trust him when it comes to my woman…" Michael said after Mark left one evening.

"You think he wanted Renè for himself?" I asked.

"Why else would he be checking on her after our breakup?" I shrugged and remained neutral in that situation. It wasn't my place to judge or throw blame around.

**

Jackson, Mississippi
December 15, 2018

As it turned out, Michael ended up getting over **one hundred thousand dollars** from the accident settlement. It shocked both of us. He was expecting only to get enough for a decently used car, but I told him that "he was going to be okay regardless." The check cleared his bank account a week later. He was so happy that he hopped up from his bed and excitedly bounced around on his good leg.

"I told you everything would work out fine…" I told him, smiling.

Do you know what he did with it? He bought his brother's fiancée a four-thousand-dollar wedding ring, got his mother a new windshield, and purchased a skateboard and a drone for himself. His brother didn't even visit him once while he was bedridden, yet he gifted him a four-thousand-dollar ring for his wife-to-be. I admired that he looked after his family, but what about me? What do you think he gave me? At first, absolutely nothing. Only when I asked did he agree to buy a new radio for my car. I wasn't the type to directly ask for money; I had an "I'll do it myself" mentality before resorting to asking for help. Some might call it pride. I was self-sufficient. Still, I wanted the man who "claimed" to love me to show it through actions without prompting. However, I was continually disappointed. I longed for tangible gestures, not just words. As time passed, I perceived more of his selfish tendencies. This wasn't the same man who gave me his shoes during the obstacle course event.

I even arranged for my mother to drive him to pick up his new car. Not only did he not offer her any gas money, but he also hesitated to pay for a simple Wendy's nugget meal for her, which I ended up paying for in the end The issue wasn't about taking advantage of him; it was about assessing his character. I had given him my time, money, affection, and energy when he was at his lowest. Yet, he acted as though buying a radio for my car was a significant imposition on his finances.

Pussy Policy #58: Never depend solely on a man for financial support.

"I want this money to last…" he said. I looked around his room at his new sixty-five-inch TV, the drone, the one thousand-dollar skateboard, and the new clothes he had bought with my eyebrows up to my hairline.

"Oh, yeah… You definitely want your money to last," I said sarcastically, glancing around the room once more…"Especially without a job or stable income…You need to be conservative."

"I am, babe."

"Hmmm. This is going to be an interesting year," I said aloud, looking up at the ceiling in annoyance. I didn't see any hope of a promise ring in sight either. I sighed heavily as I stewed while watching him squander every cent selfishly. We weren't married, so it wasn't my money, but I couldn't help but feel bitter the more time went on, and he didn't offer to buy me a new radio for my car, something that he had promised me on his own before the settlement.

Once his foot had healed to the point of him being able to walk again, I finally asked, "So, when are you going to get my radio fixed?"

He paused and looked at me in confusion while we sat in his car.

"You said that you would…" I said, looking him in the eye.

"Oh, yeah. I am," he said dismissively.

"When?"

"Next week…"

"Why not tomorrow while I'm sleeping… It's not like you're going to be at work."

"Well, I have some other things that I need to take care of…"

"Excuse me! I had other things I needed to take care of during the last couple of months while I've been in your face, but you can't do this for me?"

He paused, looking at his playlist, and looked over at me.

My agitation was visible at this point. I felt used. After months of my supporting him, he couldn't do this one thing for me.

"Wow, you are so selfish," I said, voicing my honest opinion at that point. I had nothing to lose.

"Really, babe. That's how you feel?"

"Hell yeah, that's how I feel. Even my mother reminded me that you promised me that."

"Why is your mother….. Nevermind."

My eyes narrowed as I drilled a hole in the side of his head with my gaze, daring him to continue that statement.

"Alright.. Alright.. Tomorrow it is…" he said, agitated.

"I shouldn't even have to ask…" I said honestly.

"Look, I said, 'alright!'" he said loudly.

I sat there quietly, taming my attitude before I lost my temper with him. "Look, let's just enjoy today," he finally said, realizing that I was upset. I remained silent. "Want to go see Betty Wright?" he asked, knowing exactly how to lift my spirits. "Hell, yeah!" I exclaimed, my excitement evident. My tastes in music were classic, so off we went to the concert, with him footing the bill. I was content. Later that evening, I stood on a chair, belting out the lyrics to "No Pain, No Gain" as Michael looked up at me, probably thinking I'd lost my mind. But I simply loved that song!

***

Later that week…

After I assisted him with his resume and cover letter, he secured a job in his field in Dallas, Texas. He was so thrilled that he hugged and squeezed me tightly. I shared in his excitement, seeing it as a sign that he would be relocating soon and hoping I might follow suit. However, I had no intention of 'shacking up' with a man. I would leave that to Gia. I wasn't going to pour my heart and effort into chasing a ring. If he couldn't recognize my worth, someone else would. For me, if he wanted a future together, presenting a ring was non-negotiable.

This cow's milk ain't free for much longer.

Chapter 23

POKER FACE

You think I can't see through you
But I can…
I know your thoughts.
I know your hand…
It's funny how you thought you could deceive,
You see…
I was good at poker way before you and me.
~Sovereign Jane Jenkins

Jackson, Mississippi
February 23, 2019

It looked like it would be another game night at Gia's. So, Michael and I decided to be the good Samaritans we were by stopping and buying alcohol. The grown-up drinks frequented every party, get-together, or gathering in Mississippi, in addition to someone's uncle having some moonshine in the mix.

"Hey, Y'all!" Michael said politely as we walked in.

"What's good, good people!" Gia's mom said.

Gia looked an awful lot like her mom, but in my eyes, Gia was gorgeous.

Of course, Vince had a moonshine concoction in the refrigerator. I quickly declined as Michael and I walked through the threshold of Gia and Vince's door. They had just moved into a new apartment and seemed quite smitten with each other and the new space. I personally didn't believe in shacking up with a man, but to each her own. Gia's parents were also present for that particular card game. I had met Gia's parents originally at Gia's post-graduation celebration. They were pleasant and outgoing. Gia's mom had six kids, and Gia was the oldest. I guess I could see why she moved out of her mom's house. I would have needed to change my predicament if my mother had that many offspring running around. Gia's mom appeared to be tired; it was either her weekend off from the kids or the alcohol itself kicking her under the table, but whatever it was, she didn't let it stop her from indulging in a game with her daughter on a Saturday night.

"Hey, everyone!" I said, waving at Gia from across the room. Our relationship had somewhat improved over the last few months, but it was a work in progress. I had flat ironed my hair, did my make-up, and was wearing my favorite blue easy-to-remove dress, so not even 'Miss Queen of Gia-land' was ruining my night. I had also pregamed before arriving, so I was feeling 'extra' good.

"Hey, Neka!' Gia said with surprising enthusiasm. I stared at her wide-eyed like something was wrong with her.

"It must be the alcohol," I thought silently to myself.

Vince was in the kitchen making some alcoholic elixir of sorts, but I waved at Vince through the window to the kitchen as if he weren't about to change the dynamics of the atmosphere with that one drink he was making. He was like a mixologist. Whatever it was he was making, I wanted no part of it. His drinks resulted in his guests walking sideways after leaving because of the percentage of alcohol.

"Hey, Girl! How's it going?" I asked, walking over and giving her a brief hug. I also hugged her mom and shook her stepdad's hand.

"Y'all want to play The Poker Face?"

"Sure!" I said, setting my bag on a chair and taking a seat at the dining room table with Gia and her parents. Michael sat next to me, and soon after, Vince joined the table. It was a men vs. women showdown as we delved into the card game.

"What is the top of the fishing hook called?" Gia read from a card.

Our task was to determine if the men knew the answer. If they didn't, we'd score the point. The game's objective was to maintain a good poker face and pretend we were familiar with the terms. Given that Michael frequently went fishing with his father and brother, I was almost certain he'd know. But the score was tied, and we needed a point to win. I decided to risk it, always being the daring type.

"Michael, what's the top of the fishing hook called?" I asked, feigning curiosity. From confident, Michael's expression shifted to one of surprise, probably assuming I'd back down without expecting an answer from him.

"Well, it's the top hole," he responded, sounding unsure.

Aha! His facade had slipped. He didn't actually know!

"Wrong!" Gia exclaimed. "It's called the eye!" she declared, displaying the card victoriously.

"Yes!" We girls cheered, taking a celebratory lap around the room while the guys shot reproachful glances at Michael, expecting he should've known the answer.

Michael had a decent poker face, but I was adept at discerning the truth. He seemed to accept his loss with humor.

"Whatever!" he chuckled.

Once that game concluded, we started a coin-toss game. The person correctly predicting the side on which the quarter would land would emerge victorious and richer. After parting with three dollars to Gia, I gracefully admitted defeat and moved to the couch to stay out of the fray. Gia then challenged her parents, and Vince, after mixing another drink, joined her. Michael, lighter by a few dollars himself, came and sat next to me. Being the more introverted one, I preferred to remain discreetly behind the couch as the game continued. Large gatherings often left me feeling drained.

"How are you feeling?" Michael said, lovingly rubbing my legs.

"I feel good," I said, smiling up at him. I kissed him passionately as we sat on the couch alone.

"You look good," he said with lust in his eyes.

"Thank you, baby," I said as I kissed him again. He continued rubbing my thigh, moving his hand closer towards the hem of my underwear. I tried not to squirm and giggle at his teasing, which was all it was.

"Stop it," I mouthed silently. I kissed him again, and after ending the kiss, he grabbed my hand and kissed the very top of it. I licked my lips in anticipation of later that night.

"Neka! Michael! Come join in!" I heard Gia say after she took all of her parents' quarters. I preferred to keep my quarters in my purse. I might need them for a parking meter. However, Michael removed his hand, and I stood up appearing as if nothing had happened. I frowned at the missing touch. I was enjoying Michael's game; he would always be better.

"*Stay cool, Janeka. Act natural!*" I coached myself as I looked towards Gia.

Michael stood, too, and we both walked towards the gaming table.

"Neka, you look beautiful tonight," Gia said with her eyes glossed over.

Oh, yeah. She was toasted. She must've been. I think that's the first compliment I'd ever received from her.

"Thank you," I said nonchalantly.

"What were you two talking about?" Gia asked, looking towards us.

"About Michael's moving to Texas!" I exclaimed a little too loud.

"Congratulations, my brother!" Gia said, holding up her alcoholic beverage. Her parents turned towards Michael to say their congratulations.

"Thanks, everyone!" Michael said happily. He looked so proud that he was moving on up in life. I was proud of him, but I was not going with him. Without a ring, it wasn't my place. I was NOT about to shack up with no man. I didn't care if he was about to move to Mars. I'd take a rocket ship to visit him if necessary.

Gia's mother then received a picture of her youngest child from one of Gia's younger siblings.

"Why is my child standing on my damn dining room table?" she exclaimed, glancing at her phone before quickly rising from her seat. Given that the child had special needs, her panic was understandable.

"We gotta go!" declared Gia's stepdad. They both hastened to the door, leaving behind the shot glasses and the remainder of the deck of cards. I presumed our gambling game had come to an abrupt end. I wasn't particularly fond of such activities anyway. In truth, my thoughts were preoccupied with plans involving Michael.

A smirk formed on my face as I lost myself in my musings.

"I can tell Janeka's been drinking when she starts to look Asian," Gia joked. Vince and Michael joined in her laughter. Her comment caught me off guard; I hadn't realized she'd noticed the change in my appearance. When I drank, my eyelids tended to droop. It appeared she was more observant of my habits than I'd given her credit for. I brushed the thought aside, not deeming it significant. Gia then rose from the table, the money from our card game peeking out from her bra.

"You know, this is a queen right here!" Gia said, looking at Michael in a possessive manner. It had me supremely confused. A drunk Gia was a Gia that I had to stay far away from. She was dangerous.

Michael stared at her, confused, as she approached me and grabbed my hands.

"You better treat her right," she said point blank.

"I know! I am!" Michael said.

"Because she can be mine for a night instead. I have a king-size mattress," Gia said, batting her eyelashes at Michael while Vince watched from the dining room table.

See what I mean? Dangerous!

I couldn't even look at him because my mouth was too busy sitting on the ground as I gawked at Gia. I decided to go along with it for the sake of bonding at the moment.

"She's right. You should treat me better so I won't ever leave you for her," I said with a challenging gaze.

"See! You better treat her like the queen that she is!"

"I always do!" Michael said, sticking his chest out.

"Good, because if you don't, someone else will," Gia said while getting in front of me and rubbing her ass on my thighs. *Woah! I see we're not playing games anymore.*

"I'm not worried," Michael said with a smirk on his face. "She's still coming home with me."

My face was probably beet red at that moment. I was at a loss for words, so I said nothing while grabbing her ass and rubbing slowly. I don't know if it was because I grew up with brothers or an actual past fantasy, but I was ready at that moment. So, I went for it.

"See, she's grabbing my booty. Keep your game tight, sir!"

"I'm still not worried," Michael said once again as he took a moment to observe my reaction to her teasing. Between them, I was hot and ready for something else, but I knew that would not happen at that moment. I had to suppress those emerging feelings for Gia. This situation felt like a cruel punishment.

"Oh, really?" Gia said with a challenging look towards Michael.

Uh, oh! Somebody hide the booze, because I had become thoroughly aroused. Somebody grabbed the water hose, too!

Vince cleared his throat once as we stopped and stood up straight. I evaded Vince's direct gaze. I didn't want what I felt at the moment to transfer to shame.

"Y'all want to go bowling?" Michael asked, changing the atmospheric pressure.

"Sure!" Gia and Vince agreed.

"Let me go pee before we go. The liquor is really kicking my bladder," I thought while walking towards the bathroom.

I walked into the neatly decorated space and did my business.

"I have to grab my shoes," I heard Gia say outside the bathroom door. To whom? I haven't a clue, but she opened the door as I pulled up my underwear. I was wearing a simple blue dress, so it was easy to pull them back up. I did so absentmindedly as Gia walked into the bathroom and closed the door softly. I thought nothing of it. I was still tipsy, after all. I fixed my dress as she grabbed something from the cabinet.

Maybe she had to pee, too.

I went to wash my hands as she stood back up. I looked at her through the mirror, and she had a smirk on her face. I smiled back at the sheer silliness of earlier. I turned off the running water and dried my hands on a piece of paper, averting my eyes from her, thinking maybe she'd want some privacy in her own house. I turned to my left to head to the door. There was just one problem: Gia was between me and the door. Before I could utter another word, she grabbed my face, and we kissed deeply and passionately. It was more passionate than before. Slower. I took my time breathing through every stroke of her tongue. Her lips were silky smooth. She bit me on the lip, so I put her against the sink as I lifted her dress and grabbed her full cheeks. She wore a thong. I wanted to pull it off instantly. Sitting on the sink, she pulled back and looked to her right. She turned the lock to the bathroom and looked back at me.

Well, this is not how I expected the night to go, but when life gives lemons, milk them.

I went for her mouth once more as I continued rubbing on her in every way imaginable. She was sexy as hell. I couldn't even fathom our boyfriends sitting in the next room. I couldn't stop. I didn't want to stop her. We simply got lost in each other as our spirits intertwined while our tongues danced to the rhythm of our hearts' hypnotic, sensual beats. She suddenly pulled back from the kiss and grabbed my neck. She pulled down the top of my cloth dress, exposing my left nipple. She devoured it as I tried to hold the moan in. Then, I pushed her back to return the favor. I pulled down her dress and was met with a ten-dollar bill. I pulled it out, pulled her bra down further, and circled my tongue around her areola. To keep from moaning, she buried her face in my neck. She sucked and kissed my neck as I returned the favor to her breast.

I then felt her fingers slide into my panties and draw small circles around my lips. The exact same thing Michael did earlier.

Woah! I couldn't help but think it was a plan all along.

As I came up for air, her lips searched for mine once more as I hugged her tight to me as she sat on the counter. I panted to slow my breathing as her teeth lightly bit my lips.

I expected a beer, a card game, and an innocent conversation that night, but I received much more than I bargained for.

Where did this energy come from all of a sudden...

A drunk Gia was more potent than any amount of sex serum. She was everywhere at once, and I couldn't pull myself away long enough to remember my own boyfriend sitting in the front room.

I should feel ashamed, but I didn't. Not at that moment, at least. It was like I felt vindicated in that moment because I understood that I wasn't hallucinating anything.

Gia also had a hell of a poker face. Michael had some fierce competition on his hands. I heard the door jimmy as someone tried to open it. Gia and I continued to kiss throughout the drunken stupor.

Who knew the next time an opportunity like this would come about?

The door to the spare bedroom opened, and Vince stood in the doorway, looking perplexed. I was standing close to Gia, who sat on the bathroom counter, but our clothes were securely back in place, so Vince missed most of the show.

I stepped back as Gia hopped off the counter. "Ready to bowl!" she exclaimed. I avoided eye contact with Vince, headed to the other door, unlocked it, and made my way to the living room where Michael was engrossed in his phone.

He looked up at us, seemingly unaware of the events in the bathroom. "Ready?" I asked him. He nodded and rose to his full six-foot-four height. "Ready!" he confirmed as Gia and Vince re-entered the living room. I kept my distance from Vince's gaze, ensuring I couldn't gauge his reaction.

Was he pissed? Was he agitated? I didn't really know. I didn't really want to know.

I headed outside behind Michael and slipped into the back seat of his car. Gia joined me in the back seat as Vince locked the apartment door.

Messages:
Gia: Should I apologize?

My eyebrow quirked at the message as I glanced over to her. She stared down at her phone expectantly, avoiding my gaze on purpose, awaiting my response through text.

Messages:
Me: No, apologize for what?
Gia: Good.

"Ascension" by Maxwell played as we rode in the car on the way to the bowling alley. Then, I felt her hand on my thigh.

"Uh, oh. We're going to get in trouble," I thought as I spread my legs wide, welcoming her touch.

We were playing with fire, and we both knew it. Although, I wasn't entirely that drunk by then. I had sobered up some since the bathroom incident. I could say I wanted her. I simply wanted her in a primal way. I felt stronger feelings towards her than Michael at the moment, which was a conflict of interest.

What was I supposed to do? Because what the heck! My hormones were raging uncontrollably.

I had no intention of brushing her off, so I did what any young woman would do in that situation. I grabbed her thighs and returned the favor until we arrived at the bowling alley. Who knew that beer, card games, and money exchanges would lead here? I didn't. I can say that I was happy it did. Maybe the crush would finally end.

How naive of me to think such a thing.

One thing was certain: I had to improve my poker face, especially since Vince could see me directly through his rearview mirror. I swallowed hard and shifted my gaze to the passing scenery outside the window. Guilt began to chip away at my drunken haze. Was I operating purely on lust? I certainly lusted after Gia, but was I in love with her? The guilt of cheating and lying weighed on me. If I could do what I did with Gia in the bathroom, did I truly love Michael? These questions kept swirling in my mind. Once we arrived at the bowling alley, we all dined at the bar and waited for a lane to open up. Given it was a Friday night, the alley was naturally packed.

"Y'all, I can't wait to leave Mississippi," Michael said happily.

"Maybe we could move out there one day," Vince said thoughtfully.

"Yeah, that would be awesome," Gia said.

I sat there quietly. Everyone expected me to move in with him. I wasn't. I needed a real commitment—the ring. We were nearly one and a half years in. It was past time for a real ring. I wasn't 'shacking'. I knew my worth, and I needed my own room. I liked my own space.

"When are you moving, Neka?" Gia asked.

"Once I find a job?" I said thoughtfully. *And Michael picks out a ring that fits me…*

"Well, you're a nurse. You could go anywhere and get a job. You could move in with him and look," she said.

'OH, Hell TO THE NO!' I thought to myself.

"Yeah, I could…" I said. *But I'm not. He won't want to buy the cow if the milk is constantly free. The trial period is almost up—no more test driving. I'm going to be fresh out of samples too eventually.*

Mama taught me that you had to be willing to walk away from a man at any time, but at the end of the day, I had to learn how. My fear of abandonment was triggered every time I tried to walk away after I caught him trying to remain friends with his ex.

"For my wedding, I want it to be exclusive on a sand beach in Jamaica..I'm not inviting many people…" she continued.

Hmm. I wondered why she'd say that.

I glanced towards Gia's way, "Well, I'm sure you'll make a beautiful bride," I said, glancing down at her empty ring finger. I felt a pang of jealousy. There was always this silent competition between us, yet there was still love for each other. It was an interesting dynamic.

" I really would like to move to Atlanta. It's a great place for entrepreneurs," I said out loud. I felt like I was sacrificing my dreams to follow Michael to Texas. Texas wasn't my dream.

"The strip club capital of the world?" Vince said, laughing.

"I've never been to a strip club," Michael said.

"You know it! It's legendary," I said, recalling my experience in Atlanta in my teenage years on vacation.

"I'm not into strip clubs," Michael said.

"I am," I said, grabbing my drink. "I want to throw some ones…" I said seriously.

"A night out in Atlanta doesn't sound bad…" Vince said.

"Agreed…" I said, holding my drink up higher.

"I'd much rather not be teased…" Michael continued.

But he spent time on Instagram every day liking all the models' pictures. That's not a tease?

I rolled my eyes in annoyance. I swear Michael made no sense to me sometimes.

"A night out in the A sounds fun!" Gia said. .

Surprisingly, Gia paid for my drink. I guess she's not as selfish after all… At least not when she's feeling you.

Chapter 24

THE MESSAGES

Your love is deceptive and weary.
I tried to love you dearly even though I couldn't see clearly.
The glass of your toxic love was dirty and blurry.
Leading to your cheating messages fueling my fury.
Clearly, you don't deserve me.
~Sovereign Jane Jenkins

The next morning, I woke up to go use the bathroom, and I took one look in the mirror and nearly fainted. I looked like a leopard. I had hickeys all over the left side of my neck. It looked like I was the victim of domestic abuse.

I mean, what the hell did Gia do to me? I couldn't hide this from Michael. It had scandal written all over it, literally. So, I had to do what any red-handed woman would do: come clean.

I sighed as I returned to my room and climbed into bed beside Michael. He was still drowsy but slowly waking. I lay beside him for a few minutes.

"Sleepy?" I asked him once his eyes fully opened.

"Sort of…Good morning!" he said.

He couldn't see my neck due to the darkness of the room. So, it was my chance to tell him before he saw it.

"Do you know what happened last night?" I asked.

"What do you mean?" he asked while stretching.

"I mean…Do you know what happened with Gia yesterday before the bowling alley?" I asked. His face was covered by the shadows cast by my blackout curtains.

"Y'all used the bathroom, right?" he said.

"I have to tell you something…Promise me you won't be mad."

"Spit it out…" He said, resting on his right arm.

"Something happened in the bathroom…We kissed. I went into the bathroom to use it, but then Gia walked in. I didn't think anything of it. She grabbed something out of the drawer while I pulled up my underwear. I went to wash my hands while she looked in the cabinet for something for her hair. Once I finished, I turned to leave the bathroom, facing her as she stood up at her full height, and that led to kissing. We kissed…Then, she sucked my neck…And my breasts…Just one of them, though," I said, trying to get it all out before he interrupted me, and I lost my nerve to continue.

He lay there in silence for a few minutes.

"Say something…" I said.

"Hmm. Did you enjoy it?" he asked.

"Yeah…" I said honestly.

"So, you don't have feelings for her?"

"I don't know what I feel. That came out of left field and is totally out of character for her."

"What about your character? Are you bi-sexual?"

"I don't know! All I know is that I liked it. A lot…" I said honestly.

"Do you love her?"

"No…I love you."

"Next time, how about you do it before me?"

"Huh?" I said as he stole the rest of my sentence when he climbed on top of me and kissed me. He was fully erect and needed no incentive.

"Ya nasty…" I said once he let me breathe.

"You like it…" he said.

"Wait…We need a condom."

"Babe, I told you I can't feel anything with that on."

"It's either that or nothing at all," I said, putting my foot down and about to get him off me.

He grabbed my hips, "Ok. Ok. Fine!" he said with a pout and grabbed his jeans for protection.

I showed up to work the following night with hickies on both sides of my neck. I didn't bother covering them at work since I was in a committed relationship. I was shamelessly free. I let my freak flag fly that night. Michael wasn't upset. He was actually the polar opposite of upset, but Gia reverted to the same old Gia. After the liquor wore off, she acted oblivious to that night.

Very peculiar indeed. She was no longer welcome to touch me. I wouldn't be anyone's toy, nor would I let her continue to toy with my emotions. I had feelings, too.

***

The Next Weekend…

Jackson, Mississippi
April 18, 2019

I lay in bed, waiting for Michael to return to my side. He was sleeping over at my house tonight because we were both too tired from hiking earlier to make it to his parents' house. We had settled into a peaceful flow, and I genuinely enjoyed his time. I had become so comfortable with him that it scared me. He was there for me when I needed him while I was going through hell with my father. That meant so much to me. Just his presence made me feel safer. That's what life was supposed to be, right? We had been together for six months by then. He was consistently showing up exactly when I needed him.

What more could I ask of him?

It genuinely felt like love.

Michael walked into the room after his shower. My parents were home, so we used the time to get closer to one another. I didn't expect the relationship to last that long, but he kept holding on for some reason. So, I made sure to return the favor.

After cuddling, Michael fell asleep, but I felt restless. Everything seemed to go well. It was almost too good to be true.

I eventually got up and looked around my room in my restlessness. My eyes eventually landed on Michael's phone. Something told me to go through it. It was invading his privacy, but he gave me his blessing at the beginning of our relationship, so I went to his Instagram messages.

Messages from what looked to be his ex-girlfriend's account were sent just the day before.

I immediately opened the messages.

She had sent him what looked to be pictures of food that she had cooked.

Why would she send him food pictures?

I knew 'homegirl' liked to eat and everything, being that she was built like a refrigerator, but why the hell was she texting my man food plates? And why was he replying? That was the better question.

I knew it was too good to be true...

My stomach began to hurt as my eyes started to burn from holding back the tears. He didn't deserve them.

Pussy Policy #59: You are single until you are married.

I texted Drea the messages, trying to figure out my next steps. The toughest part of possibly walking away from this relationship was the realization that I had gambled my virginity on it. I would be devastated if things didn't work out.

My daddy issues led me to make excuses for unacceptable behavior. It felt as though I was constantly walking on eggshells, afraid of doing or saying something wrong, for fear of being abandoned again. I had unresolved abandonment issues, having never sought counseling for them. I was still healing from the heartbreak caused by my fathers.

I heard Michael's snores once again. The audacity of him made me roll my eyes. Yes, I had been with Gia, but he had assured me he was over his ex. So, why was he still in touch with her? I was growing weary of the repetitive discussions. What would it take for him to understand? I wouldn't be anyone's second choice. My destiny was to be someone's one and only, and they mine—even if that meant cutting ties with Gia. It was a sacrifice I deemed worthy, and I was quite certain she would do the same. She seemed so focused on getting a ring that she often treated me poorly in front of her 'man'. I slid the phone back into my jeans pocket and climbed back into bed beside him. At three in the morning, I was seething with anger. Starting an argument now would certainly wake my parents, so I chose to remain silent tonight. But I'd confront him tomorrow. As I looked over at him sleeping so soundly, my irritation intensified. I nudged him closer to the edge of the bed with my body. It was my bed after all, and he deserved to be on the floor. Turning my back to him, I faced the wall. The ungrateful man remained undisturbed, sleeping deeply while I simmered, like a pot on a summer stove.

Bastard!

***

He awoke the next morning, and I gave him the cold shoulder. My primary concern was my bruised ego. I was hurt, feeling as though he regarded me as naive, expecting me to accept his continued contact with his ex while I remained his "girlfriend." I worried this situation would eventually lead to him cheating outright if I didn't address this absurdity. After he left my house, I waited until the afternoon to send him the screenshots of the messages between him and his ex.

Messages:

Him: You went through my phone?
Me: Wrong answer. Why are you still communicating with her?
Him: She was just showing me what she cooked...
Me: Again...Why are you still communicating with her?
Him: I was being friendly...
Me: We're done.

Contact ceased. The very next day, I tore up the childhood pictures he had left at my house. I also ripped up the card he left at the front door, threw away the flowers, and gave the chocolate to my step-dad, Mason, who loved chocolate. That was just a hint of what was to come. However, as time wore on, the weight of loneliness began to press down on me. The sadness and isolation deepened with each passing day. A week went by, and I found myself unraveling. I yearned for his presence, missed him deeply, and realized I wasn't accustomed to being single or managing everything on my own. Though I had always prized my independence, I suddenly felt lost without the familiar rhythm of a relationship.

Why didn't anyone tell me about this part?

I looked on social media, and he posted a picture of us out of town in Galveston, Texas. I texted him demanding he remove it because he didn't value me as his girlfriend. It was an anomaly that he even got me, but yet it seemed he kept testing me. I went over to Drea's house later that evening, and her mom was home sitting in her corner chair.

Tessa sat quietly and listened to me rant and vent about my relationship.

"You don't need to give him another chance…" Tessa said with finality. Drea sat beside me, watching TV while her mother lectured me.

"If you go back…. It's gonna happen again. Mark my words…" Miss Tessa said.

"I can't understand why he would throw away a perfectly good relationship…"

"Maybe it's only perfect for you…" Miss Tessa said.

"If it were perfect for him, he wouldn't risk it," she said, devastating my ego.

"Ouch…" I said, perplexed.

"The truth usually hurts when there's some evident validity attached…"

"You know you don't have to be that harsh, right?"

"I'm just trying my best to let you know the game. You're young. You're beautiful. Don't let nobody like that waste your 20s… like I did," she said, getting up from her perch on the couch.

"Has your mom always been that real?" I asked Drea.

After pausing the TV, Drea looked over to me and said, "That's child's play…" She shrugged.

If that was child's play, I didn't want to be in the vicinity during adult play because she hit me where it hurt the most.

"She does have a point, though…" Drea said while starting the movie again.

"I mean, still…she didn't have to snatch my edges like that…" I said, pouting and sinking into the seat.

"Welcome to my life…" Drea said while eating popcorn with a blank expression.

***

It had been seven whole days without any action…seven whole days without any hanky-panky… seven whole days without my old friend, who just so happened to be attached to an asshole that was still in love with his ex. I sighed, laying in my bed upside down, trying to fight the feelings…the memories…the emotional ties…And the bond that we shared. It was madness, and to think it was only the beginning of the end. I didn't want it to end. I hadn't heard from him since he left the card, flowers, and chocolate outside my front door three days prior. To be transparent, I was starting to miss him. I felt so needy and weak. I was breaking and giving in. I grabbed my phone to text him.

Me: Do you still love her?
Him: No…Her mother is dying of breast cancer, so I was trying to be supportive.
Me: Why didn't you say that?
Him: Were you actually going to listen to me and hear me out?
Me: Probably not…

Him: Exactly. She was my 'mother' for nearly five years. Letting go and saying goodbye isn't easy…Especially when you 'tryin' to love someone else.
Me: The lack of trying to communicate will wreck this relationship. You didn't even try.
Him: I know. But you didn't want to hear about her..
Me: So, why aren't you communicating directly with her mom instead?
Him: I don't want to drain her further. She's already pretty weak.

I sighed heavily. Michael didn't know that not only did I know her mother, but I grew up in church with her. I remember Renè's head just like it happened yesterday. I used to watch her father's sermons with undivided attention and conviction. It wasn't his business, though. It saddened me that the church's first lady was dying, and no one knew.

"Mama!" I said, walking into my mother's room later that evening …

"What?" Mama said while sitting down in her bathroom combing her hair.

"Have you heard that Paster Allen's wife was dying?" I asked, bewildered.

"Yes, there are rumors…Your Auntie Royce ran into her not too long ago at the hospital, and she had lost her beautiful long hair. She's bald now."

"Shit…"

"What?" Mama said

"Michael was telling the truth…He was communicating with her because her mother was dying."

"Be careful with that, Janeka. Just because her mother is dying doesn't permit him to disrespect you or y'all's relationship…" Mama said, looking up at me.

"What should I do?"

Mama smiled and looked at me. "Whatever you want to do…"

Mama never gave me real advice and always let me make my own decisions regarding dating. She had learned that I would do whatever I wanted regardless of what she said.

"Alright…" I said to Mama while walking out of her room. I grabbed my phone once I returned to my own room.

Me: Let's meet at Wingstop.
Him: I'll be there…

∗∗∗

I walked into Wingstop, and Michael was sitting at the table. One week had passed, and he looked skinnier than he had post-accident.

Why the hell was he losing weight?

"Hey," I said as I pulled out the chair.

He stood up to slide the chair behind me and ensure I was comfortable.

"Hey," he said, appearing nervous and guilty.

Once he settled in directly before me, I took a moment to assess the situation.

Was I being unfair? Was I being unreasonable? Or was I being too nice?

"Why can't you let go?" I said, finally.

He shrugged his shoulders, "It's not that simple.. You wouldn't understand…"

"Try me…" I said.

"I didn't know how…"

"DO YOU EVEN WANT ME? Because I feel like we keep having the same conversation over and over again… When does it end?" I said seriously.

"I DO WANT YOU. I love you, but she was my first love…I'm trying, ok…Her mom is dying…"

" So, go be with her," I said, fearing that he loved her more.

"It's over between us…It's not like that.. I'm simply mourning. I'm mourning Mrs. Allen and mourning you. Perhaps one day you will get it…" he said, directly appealing to the Empath in me.

I took a deep breath and cleared my mind. Could I truly see myself marrying this man? Does he even want to be married?

"Do you even want to get married?" I asked aloud.

"Of course! I was going to ask Renè to marry me before she broke up with me the last time… I don't mind getting married, but it has to be the right time. I'm locked in with you."

I leaned across the table, "Don't do this shit again. If you want her, stop wasting my time. It's my most valuable asset. You've already taken my virginity."

"Look…I want you…End of discussion…Let's try again…I want to make it up to you. Let's go on a cruise…Just you and me," he said, seeming genuinely sincere.

Now he was talking.

Michael moved to Dallas, Texas, by himself in May. I let him go alone because I still didn't have a ring. He got an apartment with two bedrooms per my request because I had never lived with anyone; I knew I would want my space and didn't plan to sleep with him.

Chapter 25

THE CURSE OF DEATH

*Death comes in the end, and it comes after defeat.
The one thing that rings true in this life is that death is guaranteed.
So, do whatever you want to do while you're free.
Because in a few years, your bones will be buried underneath.*
~Sovereign Jane Jenkins

Jackson, Mississippi
July 15, 2019

"So you're going to the funeral?" I asked Michael over the phone.

"Yeah…" he said in a cautious tone.

"And I can't go with you?" I said bewildered.

"And you are not invited…I don't think it would be the best idea. It's about her mom, after all. "You being there would be disrespectful," he said.

Just as disrespectful as her texting my man, I suppose…

"Ok…." I said, choosing not to argue with him. My presence could lead to a fight at a funeral.

"I don't want to go, honestly…," he said.

"So, when are you arriving?"

"I'll be there Saturday morning for the funeral. I know you'll be asleep all day because of your schedule, so I'll pick you up, and we can go out later Saturday night."

"Sounds good," I said, opening my phone to do a little digging. Now, up until then, I never dug for anything. I didn't care enough about an ex to worry about her. But if he thought I wouldn't be there, he had another thing coming.

***

I sat at the desk in the hospital hub, looking at the time of the funeral that morning. At that time, I worked the night shift. So, after my twelve-hour shift, I headed home, quickly changed into my black dress and heels, and rushed off to the funeral.

Was I really going to show up at a funeral uninvited? Abso-fucking-lutely. Dressed in black with my hat, I can be unpredictable when it comes to matters of the heart.

Michael wasn't aware of my attendance, but there I was, sitting at the back next to my mom and step-dad. They kept a close eye on Renè, while I watched Michael from the back of the church I had grown up attending. Renè sat between her older and younger sisters, with their brother nearby. They sat in the same order they used to when we were kids. I didn't have an issue with them, but I had to look out for my own interests.

I needed confirmation that things were truly over between them. I didn't trust Michael by that point, but neither did I have evidence of any overt cheating. So, there I sat in a pew, looking perhaps overly infatuated, but comfortably assessing the situation.

Once the funeral service ended, I walked out of the church and into the hallway. I lingered in the shadows as my mother and Mason waited to greet Pastor Allen and offer their condolences. My mother eventually exited the worship room and spotted me near the clock tower. Still, there was no sign of Michael. Finally, he appeared, emerging from the upstairs crowd. He didn't notice us, but I discreetly followed him. He headed straight for the front door.

"Michael! What are you doing here?" Mama exclaimed, catching me by surprise.

"Momma, what the fuck!" I screamed in my head. *"Shit! She got me cursing on sacred grounds…"* I sighed heavily as Michael looked back at all three of us in confusion and shock.

Now, maybe I was exaggerating, but Michael had his hair freshly done, a brand-spanking-new suit on, cologne on, and shoes that matched his suit to the T. Never had he tried to look that good during our relationship. Nor did he smell that good.

So, why today?

My agitation began to burst through the roof of the church.

"Hey," he said to my mother, visibly shaken.

"I'm here because my ex's mother passed away…" he reluctantly told my mother.

"O….K…" my mother said, visibly distrustful of his intentions.

Then he looked directly at me with my hat. I smirked and walked right past him. I needed to get to a place where I could watch him from afar around *her*. Mama foiled my initial plans. Now, I had to regroup fast.

My mother, Mason, and I walked across to the other side of the street and watched Michael walk up and hug her.

He hugged her too Goddamn long. That wasn't no 'I'm sorry you lost your mom' hug. It was an 'I'm here for you' for the long run' hug. No, the fuck you aren't gonna disrespect me like this!

I could tell he whispered something to her.

I wonder what it was….

She appeared pissed from where I was standing. It might be because of the 'un-welcomed' guest. I smirked, not feeling sorry at all for my presence. Besides, I was there for a funeral, just like everyone else.

After Michael greeted the remaining family members, he looked around until he spotted me standing there with my arms folded standing next to my parents. He walked towards me.

"Hey," he said, reaching for me. I stepped back, avoiding his touch; I felt sick to my stomach.

"Gimme a minute," I said.

"Let's go to the repass…" he said, facing his car, imploring me to get into his car.

"What did you tell her?" I asked, still standing in the parking lot.

"That you were here…What are you doing here anyway?" he said in a blaming voice.

I turned around and walked towards his car, not bothering to answer the question. It was none of his business. I opened the door and slammed it shut, not waiting for him to do it like normal.

He knew I was pissed.

"What?" he said once he got inside the car.

"Nothing at all," I said, staring directly ahead.

He sighed audibly as he pulled off, headed towards the Repass center. We sat in silence as we headed there.

Once we arrived, I jumped out of the car to find my parents. I had a feeling things might get ugly.

Once I walked into the building, all of Renè's family members sat at a horizontal table facing the rows of guests.

I sat on the opposite side of Michael instead of directly next to him. From my angle, I could see both him and Renè.

Oh yeah. Home girl was pissed. She, her sisters, and her friends were gathered at the end of the table discussing me.

Come on, people! Didn't your mother just pass? Your attention is on the wrong thing, baby boo.

I leaned back in my chair with my hands on my lap. I was visibly unmoved. I'm sure after a few minutes of deliberation, they figured out exactly who I was. My grandmother used to make her and her sisters' clothes when they were children.

I glanced at my mother, who sat beside Michael and smirked. Michael and Renè both looked visibly uncomfortable. I relaxed even further, appearing unbothered.

Pastor Allen was in the center of the table, oblivious to the storm brewing around the room. Mama visibly relaxed, daring them to try it.

The repass ended uneventfully. My mother greeted Pastor Allen before leaving. Michael and I left together, kissing in front of everyone before leaving the building.

***

Later that evening…

"Why didn't you tell me you knew Renè and her family?" he asked while lying on my bed.

"It wasn't your business," I said deadpan.

"How is it not?"

"Why did you not push for my attendance? If I'm YOUR woman. My being there shouldn't have been an issue. Yet, it was…You should have handled that a lot better."

"I hear you…but that was disrespectful. Besides, I don't know what that family will do…" he said.

"Go on…" I said.

"Yeah, but everyone was so sad at her house…They just sat there with their heads down."

I snapped my gaze his way, twitching, realizing he had gone over to their house directly after dropping me off while I was sleeping.

Why the fuck that he thought that would be ok was beyond me…OH, HELL FUCKING NO!

To keep from snapping and flat-out beating his ass around my room like a rag doll, I smiled sweetly and grabbed my cell phone to text Adrian from the gym. Two can play that game…

***

Michael and I went on the cruise three weeks later. We stopped in Cuba, Colombia, and Yucatan. We had the time of our lives. It was seven days of bliss. He bought me a new watch, paid for my massage, and bought all of my drinks. That was THE life. Maybe it could work after all.

Chapter 26

GIA'S WARNING

*The first step to true wealth is choosing yourself.
The second step to wealth is letting go of something
that damages your mental health.
The third step to wealth is finding your purpose
that serves others well.*
~Sovereign Jane Jenkins

Madison, Mississippi
June 30, 2019

After the cruise, I was still floating on cloud nine and glowing. No, I wasn't pregnant, but I felt really good. I picked up a pack of Uno Cards before heading towards Gia's job. She worked at a different hotel this time because she had gotten fired from the previous hotel due to her mouth. She had copped an attitude with one of the guests, and it didn't end well for her because the guest knew someone in upper management.

"Hey, Gia!" I said, walking into the hotel and giving her a brief hug. She was behind the counter at the front with no patrons currently. Nothing else had happened between us after bowling night. It's like she had a switch. Liquor turned the switch on. Sober Gia was 'holier than thou" and would never do anything that could be considered hedonistic. I sat down with her, and we played a few rounds of Uno.

"How are things going with Michael?"

"Things are going good," I said.

"You're bold. I would never let my man go to another state alone," she said as if I were foolish.

Pussy Policy #60: Never be afraid to have a life outside of a relationship.

I had my own goals, dreams, and aspirations independently of Michael. I saw no reason to move in with him immediately; what if the real him was abusive and controlling? I'd be isolated away from my family. I peered down at my ring finger, seeing the ring I bought instead of an engagement ring from Michael, verifying that I was making the correct decision. I saw no need to uproot my life, move to another state, and be a live-in girlfriend for a boyfriend. A husband? Definitely! But not a boyfriend who kept getting caught texting his ex every two to three months, either. I hope this relationship didn't end up being an absolute waste of time. I had gambled my most valuable asset away: my virginity.

"I'm just saying, Neka. He's a man."

"I'm aware," I said. Michael had never, ever lived by himself. He needed time to figure his life out. If he knew what he wanted, I would have had a rock on my finger after standing by him at his lowest while neither his 'best friend' nor his 'brother' could bother to come visit him while he was in bed. I smirked at her as the thought crossed my mind. If Michael's ship sank, he didn't have anyone around him to toss him a buoy if he drowned. I wasn't worried.

If he wanted to cheat, that is a character flaw I should be aware of before moving in with him. So, I was going to sit back and observe him from afar. If the conversation started getting shorter with me, I would know that it could possibly be someone else. That's ok because at the end of the day, love conquers all. If it's meant to be, it would most definitely be. If not, I was gone like the wind and would remain there for the remainder of my time on earth. No one would disrespect me and keep me as a prize at the same damn time.

"You know what Gia? I think if he were serious about me, I'd have a ring before moving in…" I said with a straight face.

"Ok," Gia said, shrugging, seemingly undisturbed by the fact that she had been living with her boyfriend for five years and still didn't have a ring. My philosophy differed. If I didn't have a ring within six months to a maximum of two years, I'd move on. Life was too short to wait for someone intent on wasting your time. I was serious about my time. Michael and I were approaching our two-year mark in a few months. If I didn't get a ring soon, I knew I'd have to decisively walk away. Honestly, given his oscillation with his ex and the disrespect he showed by visiting her house after her mother's funeral, I should have left him already. Give 'em an inch; they take a mile.

I was done giving chances, just as I was done being intimate with him. He wouldn't be getting any closer until he committed with a ring. I understood my worth and value. I deserved better than the half-commitments he presented. However, at least I benefited from the relationship. He had already invested a lot of time, energy, and money in me; if he chose to discard it all, so be it.

"Neka, men are just built differently. I'm just saying, don't leave your man alone for too long."

"Gia. Michael needs to learn independence. He's always lived with his parents. I stayed on campus alone, so I've learned self-reliance. If I moved in with him now, our differences would create clashes. He needs personal growth."

"I agree with ALL of that," Gia said, "But, Janeka, he's still a man."

I merely shrugged and glanced at the stack of cards. Lost in thought, I barely noticed Gia snap a picture of me and send it to Michael. In response, he sent her a photo: himself in sunglasses with his dress shirt partly open.

"Who is this?" I wondered aloud.

"Look at him," Gia laughed. "He's turning into a monster," she remarked, showing me the image.

I studied the photo, not sharing her amusement. He looked overly self-confident. Perhaps even arrogant. Time would tell. People could maintain pretenses only for so long. Money amplifies one's true character. I intended to be there when his real self was revealed.

"We'll see who he truly is," I thought.

"Gia, what's meant to be will be, and nothing can hinder it. You brought us together. If we're destined to last, we'll weather any storm."

I believed that. Having spoken those words, I felt compelled to trust in fate and let the universe handle things. I had reservations about moving in with someone I felt I no longer recognized. I needed certainty about who shared my bed, for now, I had so much at stake. Memories of my mother's tumultuous relationship with her first husband haunted me. I didn't want a repeat of her hardships. My fear was rooted in that history, and it felt genuine. I yearned for a genuine, good man. If that meant waiting, I'd be patient.

"Alright, Neka. Remember, if you ever want to chat, just call me."

"Thanks, girl," I said and hugged her, genuinely thankful for the talk. Time is our most valuable asset. I appreciated our time together, whether I and Michael worked out or not, even though it most likely meant that Gia and I's relationship would have to end as well. That's the gamble I took when I sent that Facebook message to Gia that day. This is what it all led to. I got a text from Michael while I was leaving Gia's job.

Him: Hey, What is your schedule for next week, and when are you coming?
Me: I have to clarify with my boss. I'll let you know.
Him: But more than likely, you're coming next weekend, right?
Me: Yes. That's the plan.

I frowned, looking down at the phone. I could have sworn we'd gone over this already…hmm…

* * *

As I packed my suitcases and gathered my toiletries, I scanned the room to ensure I wasn't leaving anything behind. I was set to spend the weekend with Michael. He wanted me in town for several events that were taking place. I was eager for the change of pace. Having started my new job just two weeks earlier, I was in need of a respite. My mind felt fatigued from endless hours of orientation and sifting through company policies. Sighing, I contemplated my outfit choices. My gaze landed on Charming, who was perched at the corner of my bed. I smiled at him; he seemed so serene at that moment.

"What would I do without Mama's baby?" I said to Charming. His head popped up happily as he heard the lightness in my voice as I petted him. He was my baby. I would be leaving him behind if I moved in with Michael. Charming couldn't stand Michael, and I think the feeling was mutual. It was weird because Charming typically loved everyone. I sighed as I gathered my packed bags and placed them into my car. I turned around to say goodbye to Charming. He was a happy puppy. He was nearly six years old but still acted like a child. He loved to be rocked to sleep and petted.

"Momma will only be gone for a few days, Charming," I said, picking up the last of my bags.

I walked out of the house and headed towards my car and climbed inside. I set the GPS to Michael's new address and started my long trek that way.

"Lord, before I pack up my life and move all the way to Texas, please reveal if he's the one that I'm supposed to be with," I said, glancing over to my Bible in the passenger seat of my car with a hopeful look as I continued on my six-hour journey.

Luckily, I had graduated from college at twenty-two years old and had options, as I could support myself. Being young, vibrant, and attractive opened many doors for me. I could either move to Texas and secure my own place, or I could stay in Mississippi and wait for Michael to propose before moving in with him. Decisions, decisions…

***

Now, I wasn't the most intuitive woman on the planet but…Michael had this guilty aura all around him. It was loud and stankin' when I stepped out of the car to greet him. I didn't hug him immediately because I was still pissed that he told me to shut up. We had gotten into an argument just two nights prior about him wanting me to block a man that had been trying to pursue me for years. He became angry and told me to shut up in response to my rebuttal regarding his still texting Rene. Maybe that was it. No one shuts me up, especially not a 'boyfriend'—a husband… maybe, but only if I'm in the wrong.

"Hey…" I said standoffishly, not leaning in to kiss him or hug him.

"What's up?" he said.

"Hey!" I said dryly.

I opened my trunk, and he removed my duffle bag. And I turned around and walked past him and towards the apartment. Of course, he knew something was off, but honestly, something was off with him too. He looked sneaky, like *a rat with the cheese that was supposed to go in the family dinner* sneaky. I wasn't ready to talk just yet.

"Hey, no hug? No kiss? What's really up?" he said, walking behind me and following my lead.

"Nope," I said as I kept walking, "We'll talk later..." I said, wanting to unwind from the long drive.

"I'm hungry. What do you want to eat?" I asked while stepping into the apartment.

"It doesn't matter..." he said while putting my bags down.

"What have you been doing?" I asked, making conversation.

He shrugged, "Waiting on you..." he said, matter of fact.

"Have you found a church home yet?" I asked while looking out of the balcony.

"No... Actually, I'm not a church-goer. Christianity isn't really my thing. How do we even know there's a God for sure?" he said.

I blinked in confusion. Had I known that, we might never have had a first date.

"Excuse me? What do you mean exactly?" I asked, growing increasingly irritated.

"I mean, my mom's a Jew, and my dad is a pseudo-Christian; I'm not sure what I believe..."

"So, you lied to me?" I said, staring at him from across the island in the kitchen.

"No... I mean, not really. I told you about my parents and that I had mixed feelings about it because of them."

"But... You said point-blank that you were Christian. Which is it?" I asked, my face reddening.

"I did identify as Christian, but I'm simply saying I'm trying to find myself and my tribe. Who says it's going to be Christian? I don't know... Time will tell," he said, as if that settled everything. I grasped the bridge of my nose and squeezed my eyes shut to keep from shouting.

"Look. It's no big deal," he said.

"Like Hell! I'm not about to be with a confused, non-Christian man. You sound like a Neanderthal. You knew that was a foundational system of belief for me. Why didn't you express that before now?"

He simply shrugged as if the conversation wasn't turning my world inside out.

"I also want to live together before getting married…To make sure that we'd get along."

I stopped rubbing my nose, and the light bulb exploded in my brain. That's what this was all about! He wanted to 'shack' knowing that was against my foundational belief, so he created this argument as a farce of manipulation to get me to agree to move in with him because he was *supposed* to be the head of the household because he paid the bills…'

I laughed out loud at the sheer stupidity of him. *He couldn't be serious.* He talked about the fact that Gia and Vince had been living together for over five years with no wedding. It was sad, but now, he sat here and opened his mouth to get me to do the same thing. *I think the fuck not.*

Pussy Policy #61: Never 'shack' with no man before marriage because you're going to naturally get on each other's nerves under one roof, which is going to cause friction, a subsequent delay in marriage, and a possible break-up if that person decides that they no longer want you. Also, never remain a girlfriend for too long; set a timeline and stand on it.

He knew my timeline was two years, and we were approaching our second anniversary fast.

Ah.. He wants the milk and not the cow. He wants to continue the free trial without commitment. He wants the family Netflix password without payment. Definitely an "I think not" situation.

"Ok," I said with a smirk, finally seeing his angle but not pointing it out.

"Ok…" he said, bewildered.

"Yes. What do you want to eat?" I asked before I said something that I couldn't take back.

At least all my meals were free since he wanted to keep getting the kitty, but soon, that would be completely off of the table until…

***

We ended up at a seafood restaurant, which was my favorite, and planned to attend his friend's party that night. I felt grossly unhappy because I felt like we should have been engaged by then, but there was still no sign of a ring. I sighed as I sat there at the party. The introvert in me wasn't interested in talking and was ready to go. We ended up leaving the party early and stopping for Sonic on the way home.

"Do you feel as if you settled with me?" he asked out of the blue while waiting on the food.

"In some ways," I said honestly. "You?" I asked, looking over at him.

"In some ways…" he said, mimicking me.

"Be serious!" I said with a straight face.

"I feel like any time you settle down, you're settling for something. It's like you must go through a perpetual hell to get to heaven. Like you must deal with the fire and brimstone before the cozy fire on a snowy day. I feel like my accident was my hell. I hope it ends there," he said, looking straight ahead.

"Me too…" I said as the hostess approached the car and handed us the food.

Once we made it home, we had sex like it was the first time all over again, and just like the first time, he fell into a deep coma-like sleep. I sat up to pee and spotted his phone. I looked at him and looked at the phone once more.

Should I? Well, of course! Ain't no privacy when it comes to my heart.

I picked up the phone, walked into the closet, sat on the floor, and scrolled until I reached an unfamiliar name. *Who the fuck is Kendal?*

***

The Three As to Healthy Dating:

Abstinence

Attention

Apprehension

Make men wait an undisclosed amount of time before having sex: practice ABSTINENCE. The same willpower required while waiting for you is the same restraint needed in marriage for fidelity. While they are waiting, watch them closely and pay ATTENTION. Observe whether their actions match their words. If the actions and words don't align, it's manipulation. Don't get caught in his web. Remember, actions always speak louder than words. There's immense power in the art of abstinence because it allows you to see clearly without being blinded by seduction, lust, romance, or the artificial chemical cocktail in your brain that mimics love. This clarity reveals reality, and your chances of being taken advantage of dramatically decrease when you're thinking lucidly because you can see through the smoke screen. Understand your partner's intentions: this is about APPREHENSION. He will reveal them when the right questions are posed. In essence, set strong boundaries and adhere to them rigorously in all types of relationships. So, I implore you to do some self-reflection. Now, YOU tell me: What's your "Pussy Policy"?

PUSSY POLICY

1. _____
2. _____
3. _____
4. _____
5. _____
6. _____
7. _____
8. _____
9. _____
10. _____
11. _____
12. _____
13. _____
14. _____
15. _____
16. _____
17. _____
18. _____
19. _____
20. _____

ABOUT THE AUTHOR

Sovereign Jane Jenkins was born in Jackson, Mississippi—a place where you come to know of Emmett Till and Jesus Christ before reaching the age of five. She was the youngest of three children, raised by her mother and stepfather. However, after discovering that she wasn't his biological daughter, her stepfather abandoned both her and her brother, despite having raised them during their formative years. He soon after remarried, leaving behind the memories of the children that weren't his own. Despite her tumultuous childhood, Jane's school age years were spent on the drill team in middle school ,and she later joined the JROTC in high school. Excelling academically, she graduated with a 4.4 GPA, then pursued her Bachelor of Science in Nursing at the University of Southern Mississippi, earning her a degree and a distinguished scholar of Magna Cum Laude with a minor in Spanish in 2018. Outside of writing, Jane enjoys running, hiking, socializing with friends, vacationing in Europe, reading new books, and acquiring new languages. Both her biological parents reside in Mississippi, and she cherishes spending holidays surrounded by family and friends. She frequently reads works by her favorite authors like Napoleon Hill, Paulo Coelho, and Theodora Taylor. As she continues to write, she remains in the state of Georgia; she has a keen interest in aiding others with the lessons that she has learned along her journey.

Hey! Keep in Touch!

Instagram: Sovereign_jane

Facebook Profile: Sovereign Jane Jenkins

Facebook Group: Sovereign Thinkers: Establishing Boundaries and Fortifying Self Respect

Tikitok: Sovereign_jane

Reddit: u/Sovereign_jane

LinkedIn: Sovereign Jane Jenkins

Email: sovereignjane95@gmail.com

Youtube: Sovereign Thinkers